ROSE ,
KENNEDY'S
FAMILY ALBUM

GRAND CENTRAL
PUBLISHING

NEW YORK   BOSTON

ROSE
KENNEDY'S
FAMILY ALBUM

From the

FITZGERALD KENNEDY
PRIVATE COLLECTION
1878–1946

FOREWORD BY
CAROLINE KENNEDY

ARRANGED AND EDITED BY THE
JOHN F. KENNEDY
LIBRARY FOUNDATION

Grand Central Publishing
Hachette Book Group
237 Park Avenue
New York, NY 10017

www.HachetteBookGroup.com

Printed in China

IMA

First Edition: October 2013
10 9 8 7 6 5 4 3 2 1

Grand Central Publishing is a division of Hachette Book Group, Inc.
The Grand Central Publishing name and logo is a trademark of Hachette Book Group, Inc.

The Hachette Speakers Bureau provides a wide range of authors for speaking events. To find out more, go to www.hachettespeakersbureau.com or call (866) 376-6591.

The publisher is not responsible for websites (or their content) that are not owned by the publisher.

Library of Congress Cataloging-in-Publication Data
Rose Kennedy's Family Album: from the Fitzgerald Kennedy private collection, 1878-1946 / foreword by Caroline Kennedy, First edition.

    pages cm

    ISBN 978-1-4555-4480-6 (hardcover)—ISBN 978-1-4555-4481-3 (ebook) 1. Kennedy family—Pictorial works. 2. Kennedy, Joseph P. (Joseph Patrick), 1888-1969—Pictorial works. 3. Kennedy, Rose Fitzgerald, 1890-1995—Pictorial works. 4. Kennedy, John F. (John Fitzgerald), 1917-1963—Pictorial works. 5. Kennedy, Robert F., 1925-1968—Pictorial works. 6. Kennedy, Edward M. (Edward Moore), 1932-2009—Pictorial works. 7. Presidents—United States—Pictorial works. 8. Politicians—United States—Pictorial works I. Kennedy, Caroline, 1957-

    E843.K492 2013

    973.922092'2—dc23   2012051197

BOOK DESIGN BY SHUBHANI SARKAR

The Kennedy family in Bronxville, New York, 1937.
Left: Joe, Pat, Jack, Jean, and Eunice.
Right: Bobby, Kathleen, Teddy, Rosemary, Joe Jr., and Rose.

CONTENTS

A NOTE ON THE PHOTOGRAPHS

IX

FOREWORD BY CAROLINE KENNEDY

XI

CHAPTER 1

THE EARLY YEARS

3

CHAPTER 2

THE BOSTON YEARS

31

CHAPTER 3

THE BRONXVILLE YEARS

87

CHAPTER 4

THE EMBASSY YEARS

199

CHAPTER 5

THE WAR YEARS

263

CHAPTER 6

POLITICAL BEGINNINGS

321

ACKNOWLEDGMENTS

345

CREDITS

347

A NOTE ON THE PHOTOGRAPHS

The photographs in this book were selected from the larger Kennedy Family Collection, which is preserved at the John F. Kennedy Presidential Library and Museum in Boston. The entire collection comprises more than fifty albums and scrapbooks. The staff at the John F. Kennedy Library Foundation chose the images in this book from approximately twelve thousand photographs, the majority of which have never before been published.

In accordance with the family's wishes, all the proceeds of this book will be shared by the Joseph P. Kennedy Jr. Foundation and The John F. Kennedy Library Foundation.

The Joseph P. Kennedy Jr. Foundation is dedicated to improving the lives of those with intellectual disabilities. The John F. Kennedy Library Foundation supports the educational mission of the John F. Kennedy Presidential Library and Museum and seeks to inspire new generations to public service.

FOREWORD

Looking at these photographs is a trip through time and a journey through family history. It gives me the chance to examine the childhood faces of adults I have known and loved, and to see the resemblances among the children and grandchildren, aunts, uncles, and cousins who have been my lifelong companions. This book tells a story common to many Americans: immigrants making good in a couple of generations, the proud photographs of a growing brood, the beginning of leisure time, new cars and vacations, traveling to Europe, and the young men in uniform. It's all part of the American Dream—and that's before our story even really begins.

The people who set this in motion were my grandparents Joseph P. Kennedy and Rose Fitzgerald Kennedy. And because this is a chronicle of the domestic side of their life, it is really my grandmother whose spirit comes through the pages. Grandma was famously organized, keeping index cards on each of her children—their health, their habits, their school accomplishments—even their shoe sizes. She ran the growing household with help, but also with discipline and an incredible number of matching outfits.

Each summer when the children are lined up on the beach, there seems to be another person in the picture. Each time my great-grandparents come to stay, they are wearing more curious bathing costumes and old-fashioned attire, while my grandparents become more elegant and fashionable as the years go on.

More important, she raised nine children who changed the world in which they lived. These pictures don't tell that story but they do reveal some of the qualities that made it possible—intense loyalty, and deep affection, the importance of faith, joy in seeing the world together and experiencing all it has to offer.

As a public figure, Rose Kennedy has sometimes been described as overly pious, or emotionally distant. But to her children and grandchildren, those descriptions are far off the mark. Growing up, there was never any doubt in our minds who was the heart and soul of our family, the most fun, most curious, most understanding, most open-minded, most self-disciplined, most practical, and most political adult we knew—Grandma.

At dinner the night after her death at age 104, Uncle Teddy asked us to offer reminiscences. It was a special evening of memories, full of tears and laughter and lessons on life. One grandchild described the time his car was stuck on the beach, and Grandma was the only one who knew how to save it from the incoming tide. Others spoke about her fierce Irish pride, developed at a time when "No Irish Need Apply" signs were common in Boston business windows. We all remembered getting up early to go to Mass with her, and saying the Rosary—the Glorious Mysteries were her favorites. People recalled listening to Grandma recite "The Midnight Ride of Paul Revere" and being called on to do the same, or being terrified of the countless math problems and American history quizzes she posed at meals. I recalled her asking to borrow my bicycle at age 85 and riding away up the driveway.

Grandma loved to look pretty and dress well. She loved being outdoors and took long walks after lunch and dinner. If you were lucky enough to walk with her, she would give you a peppermint from her purse. She loved politics—from the presidency down to the precinct level—and believed that everyone should serve their country.

Grandma always wanted to know the latest news, preferably from the people who were making it. She never gave up practicing her French and German. She had a deep devotion to the Blessed Mother, and drew immense strength and solace from her faith. Most of all, she loved her children—she delighted in their jokes, she was part of their daily lives, she wrote or called or visited them every day, and made sure they checked on each other.

My grandparents had a special place in their hearts for their daughter Rosemary, who was born with an intellectual disability at a time when children like her were often hidden. One of the remarkable things about this photo collection is how obvious it is that Rosemary was part of family life in every possible way. In her younger years, she usually sits between Jack and Kathleen, the siblings closest to her in age, and later she is pictured most with Eunice, who devoted her own life to improving the lives of people like her special sister.

My favorite photo is the one of Grandma on her wedding day. She looks so beautiful in her satin lace dress, her delicate veil, and the huge bouquet of flowers. It's a wedding from a bygone era yet she kept the same radiance all her life. I also love the pictures of all the children in the rowboat wearing bandanas, looking like they are having a terrible time. But the most poignant are the photos of my father and my Uncle Joe in uniform because they bring home the eternal pain and loss of war.

My grandparents provided the love and security that allowed their children to reach great heights. For my generation, Grandma remained the center of our family. Returning to Hyannis Port in the summer was a chance to reconnect with her, to be reinspired by her faith and her sense of fun, to draw strength from the rituals that she had created and to pass them on to our own children.

To those of us who knew her, she sparkled—and the world she created was one we felt fortunate to inhabit. For people who never met Rose Fitzgerald Kennedy, I hope these photos will convey some of her intangible gifts and help us all to give our own families as much as she gave to hers.

—CAROLINE KENNEDY

"God made the world and made us to live in it for a while. We owe Him infinite thanks and obligations and duties. Surely among these is the appreciation of the delights of life: the beauties of nature, the places and people of this earth, the pleasures of good company, the grace of laughter, the scent of a flower, the sounds of music, the rhythm of dancing, the infinite satisfactions of true love—all those joys that are there for us to claim as human beings created by God's will and endowed by His wisdom with capacities to enjoy this life. Birds sing after a storm: why shouldn't people feel as free to delight in whatever sunlight remains to them? If more people were more thankful for what they have, instead of mournful for what they have not, much good would come to the world."

ROSE FITZGERALD KENNEDY

ROSE KENNEDY'S
FAMILY ALBUM

I should appreciate it if no one remove pictures
from this book. If you do so, it will not be
so interesting for other people.

Personally, I should like to keep all the pictures
to look at myself, because as you know we lost
all the moving pictures of you children.

Many of these pictures have been lost in the past,
due to the clamor of newspapermen, so please do
not remove any more.

Thank you.

Rose Kennedy

Rose saved thousands of family photographs during her long life. As the Kennedy family's stature grew from 1938 onward, so did the requests for photographs. Soon Rose discovered much to her dismay that photographs would routinely go missing, so she had the above note typed and placed on the front page of her photo albums. The loss of "all the moving pictures of you children" is a reference to a warehouse fire in the 1950s that destroyed the Kennedy family home movies.

Rose with her younger sister and brother,
Agnes and Thomas, circa 1900.

CHAPTER

1

THE EARLY
YEARS

Joseph Patrick Kennedy and Rose Elizabeth Fitzgerald came from proud Irish stock, and that would have an effect on their family's identity, work ethic, and ambitions for generations to come. All four of their paternal grandparents—Patrick Kennedy and Bridget Murphy, and Thomas Fitzgerald and Rosanna Cox—emigrated from Ireland to Boston in the late 1840s. They were part of a mass exodus caused by the Irish Famine, a potato crop failure which lasted for five years and killed nearly one million people while sending another two million into exile. Many Irish who left for America didn't survive the voyage across the Atlantic Ocean, dying from disease on board ships or languishing at the quarantine station in Boston Harbor. But the families of Joseph and Rose were among the fortunate survivors who endured and flourished, and that durability became part of the family's legacy.

The nineteenth-century Irish immigrants coming off the boats in Boston Harbor believed they were stepping into the Promised Land. They were often startled to encounter rampant anti-Irish discrimination among nativist Bostonians. It was an unpleasant and ugly truth that many Bostonians, even those descended from the early Puritans who came to Massachusetts in search of religious freedom, were intolerant of Irish, Catholics, and immigrants in general. That prejudice often had a violent and tragic outcome, as Irish newcomers were physically harassed, their homes and churches burned, their children not welcome at Yankee schools or social events. "No Irish Need Apply" ads ran in Boston newspapers frequently. In addition to lawmakers seeking to restrict their civic and religious freedoms, Irish families faced social discrimination, including limited opportunities for employment and intolerance in schools and other parts of society. The Kennedys and the Fitzgeralds had a heightened sense of pride and purpose in overcoming such trials and tribulations on their road from poverty to prosperity.

Joseph P. Kennedy, born in East Boston on September 6, 1888, came from this type of family. He was the son of Mary Augusta Hickey and Patrick Joseph Kennedy, an important figure in Boston's Irish community whose parents were of the Famine generation. Known as P.J., Joe's dad had risen from common laborer to highly successful businessman, buying a run-down saloon in Haymarket Square, then purchasing two more taverns and eventually becoming a wholesale liquor distributor. He was instrumental in the organization of two Boston

A rare, undated photograph of Mary Augusta Hickey Kennedy.

financial institutions, the Columbia Trust Company and the Sumner Savings Bank. Early on, P.J. had also entered politics, serving in the Massachusetts House of Representatives and Massachusetts Senate. But his enduring influence was in his unofficial capacity as a "ward boss" in East Boston's Ward Two, helping to organize the Irish community into a powerful political force. P.J. held sway in East Boston for more than thirty years.

Joe Kennedy grew up in East Boston with his younger sisters, Loretta (born 1892) and Margaret (born 1898). Another brother, Francis, born three years after Joe, did not survive infancy. Joe attended Catholic schools until the eighth grade, when he enrolled in the prestigious Boston Latin School, a college preparatory academy in the Boston Public School System. He was captain of the baseball and the tennis teams, a star on the basketball team, and class president his senior year. He graduated from Boston Latin in 1908 and entered Harvard University, one of a handful of Irish Catholics admitted to study there, eventually earning a bachelor of arts degree in 1912. That fall, Joe became an assistant

state bank examiner for Massachusetts, the first step in a career that would bring him great wealth.

In his last years at Harvard, Joe began courting Rose Fitzgerald, daughter of Boston Mayor John F. (Honey Fitz) Fitzgerald and the former Mary Josephine Hannon. Rose, their eldest child and first daughter, was born on July 22, 1890, in Boston's North End, a bustling neighborhood on the city's waterfront filled with merchants, sailors, peddlers, and immigrants, mainly Irish, Jewish, and Italian. Honey Fitz and Mary Josephine would have five more children: Agnes, Eunice, Thomas, John Jr., and Frederick.

At the end of the nineteenth century, politics was a sure way for Irish immigrants to rise from their humble surroundings and climb the American ladder of success. Like Joe Kennedy, Rose was born into a political family. Her father, John, was on the Boston Common Council and in the Massachusetts Senate, and was a U.S. congressman from 1895 to 1901, when Rose was just a child. When Rose was fifteen, Honey Fitz was elected mayor of Boston, serving in 1906–1907 and 1910–1913. Her graduation from Dorchester High School in June 1906 was front-page news in the Boston newspapers as Mayor Fitzgerald proudly gave Rose her diploma.

Because her mother was not comfortable in a political role, Rose served as hostess at many of her father's political events, an experience that would prepare her for a life as the daughter and mother of politicians and as the wife of a prominent public

(OPPOSITE) The Kennedys and the Fitzgeralds vacationing in Old Orchard Beach, Maine, circa 1907. P.J. (second to the left), Rose (third to the left), Honey Fitz (fourth to the left), and Joe (second to the right).

figure. Rose's father was regarded as one of the most popular and colorful Boston politicians in the city's history. Nicknamed "Honey Fitz" because of his sweet singing voice, Fitzgerald once said, "When I was mayor of Boston, I learned that everywhere a mayor went, he had to make a speech, and no one really wanted to hear a speech every time, so I sang." His favorite song, "Sweet Adeline," became the unofficial anthem of his many political campaigns.

Rose had been accepted at Wellesley College during her junior year in high school, but Honey Fitz consulted with Catholic Archbishop William O'Connell, and instead enrolled her in the Academy of the Sacred Heart in Boston. At first, Rose was unhappy with the decision, but she eventually grew fond of the convent school, and the religious training she received there became the foundation of her life of faith. She later studied French and German at the Blumenthal convent boarding school in the Holland countryside near the city of Aachen, Germany, or as the French called it, Aix la Chapelle.

Like Joe, Rose often felt the sting of anti-Irish sentiments in Boston, where Irish Catholics like her were excluded from joining social clubs run by proper Bostonians of inherited wealth and status. So in 1910, having traveled to Europe, and being fluent in foreign languages and an accomplished pianist, Rose formed the Ace of Clubs, a group for women who had studied abroad and were interested in history and current events. Before long, the Ace of Clubs had became a fashionable group with a serious purpose, performing social work, hosting afternoon socials for charity, and fostering intellect while giving Irish Catholic women a venue for meeting and networking.

As the scions of important and influential men, Rose and Joe had grown up in the same circles, and had even spent a summer vacation together in Old Orchard Beach, Maine, when they were children. In their adolescent years, Joe started accompanying Rose to dances and parties; he would later say that he was "never seriously interested in anyone else." But after Rose's successful debut in Boston society and Joe's graduation, the courtship became more firmly established despite the disapproval of Honey Fitz, who thought Joe was not good enough for his daughter. Honey Fitz was finally convinced that Joe was worthy of Rose when Joe became the president of Columbia Trust, the youngest bank president in the country at age twenty-five.

Later, Rose could not recall Joe's actual proposal and thought it was probably more a question of "when we get married" versus "will you marry me?" Rose and Joe's engagement was announced in the Boston newspapers on June 21, 1914. "Few girls have had the social experience Miss Fitzgerald has had," reported the *Boston Globe*, also citing her academic and musical achievements. Joe was described as having "won high honors both in the classroom and on the baseball field" at Boston Latin and Harvard, and his prowess as a young business leader was also noted.

Patrick Joseph (P.J.) Kennedy, circa 1878.

"As bartender, host, and proprietor, P.J. Kennedy found himself in the middle of East End [East Boston] news, gossip, celebrations, hopes and fears, troubles and tragedies. He was a good listener, knew how to keep confidences, and had a compassionate spirit. He helped people with loans, gifts, and advice. Often he passed the word on to somebody that so-and-so needed this or that and P.J. Kennedy would appreciate it, asking nothing in return but goodwill. Everyone knew that he was an honorable man, and everyone respected him. He was 5 feet 10 inches, with a brawny physique, blue eyes, a rain-washed, rosy complexion, reddish hair, and a handlebar mustache that swooped gracefully, adding to his air of composure and dignity. Predictably, he became a political force in East Boston. And before long, he was the most influential figure of that whole region of the city."

ROSE'S DESCRIPTION OF P.J. KENNEDY

P.J. Kennedy, circa 1890s.

John Francis (Honey Fitz) Fitzgerald, circa 1883.

“ My father, on the contrary, and perhaps because of being denied the credentials of an education, retained his appetite for knowledge and became an avid reader. He had wonderful azure blue eyes…and boundless curiosity, so he read everything within reach: books, magazines, and, of course, many newspapers…

And what he read, he remembered. He had a stupendous memory for facts and figures, points of law, historical facts, quotations, anecdotes, and, of course, anything to do with Boston—all of great advantage to him in his political speechmaking and in debating an opponent. He had a famous ability to talk about anything persuasively, cogently, and with swarms of facts seemingly produced from the thin blue. ”

ROSE’S DESCRIPTION OF HER FATHER, JOHN “HONEY FITZ” FITZGERALD

Honey Fitz, the year he was elected to the United States
House of Representatives, 1894.

"He [P.J.] and my father had been friends, or at least close acquaintances, for a long time. Temperamentally they were opposites, and I suppose they must have grated on each other's nerves at times. But they had many things in common too: their immigrant background, the early deaths of their fathers, the personal determination, foresight, and hard work that raised them to their positions, and, of course, a sophisticated understanding of politics. I'm sure they understood each other and each in his way liked and admired the other."

ROSE'S DESCRIPTION OF THE RELATIONSHIP
BETWEEN HONEY FITZ AND P.J.

Honey Fitz and P.J. on horseback while vacationing in
Asheville, North Carolina, circa 1895.

Joseph Patrick Kennedy, circa 1892.

Rose and her younger sister, Agnes, circa 1894.

(RIGHT) Joe with his younger sister Loretta, circa 1895.

(BELOW) Joe with younger sisters, Margaret (middle) and Loretta, circa 1900.

"She had dark Irish looks, with a fine complexion, and a small, lithe, trim figure, which she never lost. From the time she married to the end of her life (at the age of ninety-eight), her weight seldom varied much from 115 pounds. She was fine-boned and finely proportioned, standing only about 5 feet 3 inches but seeming taller because of the dignity of her bearing."

ROSE'S DESCRIPTION OF HER MOTHER,
MARY JOSEPHINE HANNON FITZGERALD

Mary Josephine Hannon Fitzgerald, circa 1901.

(ABOVE) The Fitzgerald family, circa 1907. Back row: Agnes, Thomas, John Jr., and Rose. Front row: Mary Josephine, Frederick, Honey Fitz, and Eunice.

(OPPOSITE) An undated photograph of P.J. and his wife, Mary Augusta, and their daughters, Margaret (left) and Loretta.

Mayor John Fitzgerald and Rose view a parade outside
Boston City Hall, circa 1910.

"I well remember my first trip to Palm Beach in the winter of 1911. I was a debutante and a trip to Palm Beach was supposed to be a delight in those days. It meant new summer clothes to wear in the hot climate by day and more evening clothes than were customary for Boston. There was a new atmosphere there, new friends, and hopefully new beaux. So my father said that he would give me this wonderful treat. But Joe had asked me to the Junior Prom at Harvard and even arranged for one of his roommates to invite a friend of mine, thinking it would be easier for me to get permission to go. But alas for our plans, my father remained adamant about my going to Palm Beach. My mother said I had better go because I would never get a chance to go again probably. So, I took the long forty-two-hour ride on the train, hoping, praying, all the way, that a disaster would hit the city of Boston—a big snowstorm, a tremendous fire, so that the Mayor would be called home, and I could go to the Junior Prom, but nothing like that happened. And fate is so cruel, because every year since then, I have gone to Palm Beach—but never have I been to a Junior Prom. "

ROSE'S DESCRIPTION OF HER FIRST TRIP TO PALM BEACH

Rose Elizabeth Fitzgerald, the year of her official debut
to Boston society, 1911.

"My debut was not lavish, at least by the standards of those times. It was a
beautiful reception and tea at our home in Dorchester. Though it was the dead of
winter, my parents had turned the house into a bower of roses for me. There were
other flowers, too, as accents, and ferns and palms and garlands, but roses were
the motif of the day."

ROSE'S DESCRIPTION OF HER DEBUT

Joseph P. Kennedy in uniform as the colonel of the drill regiment while at the prestigious Boston Latin School, 1908.

Joseph P. Kennedy, the year he graduated from Harvard University with a bachelor of arts, 1912.

"Joe Kennedy was tall, thin, wiry, freckled, and had blue eyes and red hair. Not dark red, orange red, or gold red, as some Irish have, but sandy blond with a lot of red lights in it. His face was open and expressive, yet with youthful dignity, conveying qualities of self-reliance, self-respect, and self-discipline. He neither drank nor smoked, nor did I. He was a serious young man, but he had a quick wit and a responsive sense of humor. He smiled and laughed easily and had a big, spontaneous, and infectious grin that made everybody in sight want to smile too. Even then, he had an aura of command, an attitude of being competent to take charge of any situation."

ROSE'S DESCRIPTION OF HER HUSBAND, JOE KENNEDY

Joseph P. Kennedy, president of the Columbia Trust
Company in Boston, circa January 1914.

Rose's official engagement photograph, circa 1914.

Rose with Joe Jr., Rosemary, and Jack,
circa 1919.

2

THE BOSTON YEARS

The excitement and anticipation of the Kennedy-Fitzgerald wedding throughout the summer of 1914 was tempered by political upheavals taking place across Europe. A week after Rose and Joe announced their engagement, Franz Ferdinand, archduke of Austria, was assassinated on June 28, unleashing a growing tension in Europe and Asia that ultimately erupted into conflict. Soon Germany, France, Britain, Serbia, Russia, and Japan were all embroiled in declarations of war, and armies began mobilizing across frontiers. U.S. president Woodrow Wilson quickly announced America's neutrality, but there was growing unease and tension that the United States would be drawn into the conflict, and indeed, it ultimately was.

On October 7, 1914, Rose Fitzgerald and Joseph Kennedy were married in a private ceremony before the two families and a few select friends, officiated by William Cardinal O'Connell in the chapel of his official residence. Rose wore "white duchesse satin, with rose point lace trimming and garniture of silver and pearls," wrote the *Boston Globe*. After a three-week honeymoon in the popular resort town of White Sulphur Springs, West Virginia, with side trips to Philadelphia, Atlantic City, and New York City, the couple settled at 83 Beals Street in the Boston suburb of Brookline, in a house Joe had purchased in August. The three-story house was on a street lined with sycamore trees, only a few blocks away from the local school and a short walk to both the trolleys and St. Aidan's Catholic Church.

In Brookline, Rose set about creating a home that would be the center of their family life. They bought their first car together, a shiny black Ford Model T, decorated their home, and socialized with friends from college. Rose and Joe's first year together established vacation routines, and these getaways would remain important throughout the years of their marriage. From the beginning, there were winter vacations in Poland Springs, Maine, and summer vacations in the seaside towns of Hull and Cohasset, located along the south shore of Massachusetts.

It was during their first summer vacation at a rented house in Hull that Rose gave birth to their first child, Joseph Patrick Kennedy Jr., on July 25, 1915. Rose's father, Honey Fitz, greeted the news with his usual aplomb and promptly set forth the newly born child's future: "Well…of course he *is* going to be President of the United States, his mother and father have already decided that he is going to Harvard, where he will play on the football and baseball teams and incidentally take all the scholastic honors. Then

Rose Fitzgerald Kennedy and Joseph Patrick Kennedy
on their wedding day.

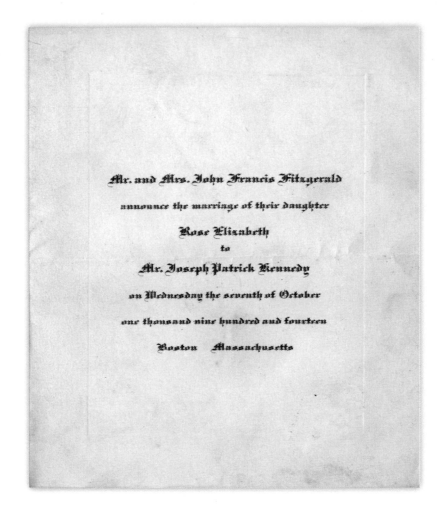

Mr. and Mrs. John Francis Fitzgerald

announce the marriage of their daughter

Rose Elizabeth

to

Mr. Joseph Patrick Kennedy

on Wednesday the seventh of October

one thousand nine hundred and fourteen

Boston   Massachusetts

he is going to be a captain of industry until it's time for him to be President for two or three terms. Further than that has not been decided."

On May 29, 1917, at about three o'clock in the afternoon, Rose gave birth to a second son, John Fitzgerald Kennedy, named in honor of his maternal grandfather. He was the first Kennedy child born at the 83 Beals Street home, to be followed by Rose Marie (Rosemary), born on September 13, 1918, and Kathleen Agnes (Kick), born on February 20, 1920.

Although 83 Beals Street "was a nice old wooden-frame house with clapboard siding; seven rooms, plus two small ones in the converted attic, all on a small lot with a few bushes and trees," it became apparent to Rose and Joe shortly after Kick's birth that they had outgrown their first home. In

March 1920, Joe purchased a larger house designed in the Queen Anne style, three blocks away at 131 Naples Road. The second Kennedy home was originally built in 1897 and had twelve rooms, turreted windows, a wraparound porch, and a garage. Most important, it was large enough to accommodate a rapidly growing family with the arrivals of Eunice Mary, born on July 10, 1921; Patricia (Pat), born on May 6, 1924; and Robert Francis (Bobby), born on November 20, 1925.

Rose was a very disciplined and organized woman. In order to keep track of the many needs of their growing family, she maintained note cards for each of the children in a small wooden file box and made a point of writing down everything from a doctor's visit to the shoe size they had at a particular

35

age. During the school year the children attended the Edward Devotion School, a public school near their home. Starting in 1924, Joe, wishing to expose his two eldest sons to the patrician Anglo-Protestant families of Boston, nicknamed the Brahmins, would send Joe Jr. and Jack to the Dexter School, a private boys' school also located in Brookline.

At the end of each school year, the Kennedy children embarked on their summer vacation, either in Hull or Cohasset, and by 1925, Hyannis Port on Cape Cod, where they enjoyed swimming, sailing, and playing touch football. The Kennedy children played hard, and they enjoyed competing with one another.

As president of Columbia Trust, Joe worked diligently to cultivate connections, maintaining good relations with his working-class client base but always seeking new links to Boston's business elite. His entry into that circle was confirmed on the day of Jack's birth, when he was elected to the Board of Trustees of the Massachusetts Electric Company, New England's leading public utility at the time.

Joe's connection with fellow board member Guy Currier, a prominent Boston lawyer and counsel for Bethlehem Steel, would lead to his next position in October 1917 as the assistant general manager at Bethlehem Steel's Fore River Shipyard in Quincy, Massachusetts. By then, the Fore River Shipyard was one of the largest shipyards in the country and was booming with military orders as a result of the United States' entry into World War I. It was during his tenure at Fore River that Joe would first meet—and sometimes clash with—Franklin D. Roosevelt, then U.S. assistant secretary of the navy.

When World War I ended in November 1918, Joe realized that there would not be the same challenges or prospects with Bethlehem Steel. He returned to finance and, utilizing his connections from the Massachusetts Electric Company, joined the prestigious brokerage firm of Hayden, Stone and Company in 1919. When his mentor, Galen Stone, retired in 1923, Joe decided to leave the firm and establish himself as "Joseph P. Kennedy, Banker." In this capacity, Joe offered a range of financial services based on the knowledge and skills he had developed working with Stone.

In 1926, Joe engineered a deal with a syndicate of Boston investors to buy the company Film Booking Offices (FBO), a producer and distributor of silent films, thereby entering into the burgeoning movie industry. He spent the next year getting FBO on a solid business footing, and creating a finance company, Cinema Credits Corporation, for which Joe tapped into his many contacts in the financial world. At the same time he imposed a fiscal discipline on FBO that was new to the company and, indeed, Hollywood.

Marking his new position as a movie executive, Joe made a major move personally, taking the Kennedy family from Boston to the New York suburb of Riverdale in the fall of 1927.

"Married at the Cardinal's chapel at nine o'clock on Wednesday, October seventh. Wedding pictures taken at home before and after the ceremony. Bouquet of white orchids and lilies of the valley. Pictures for papers snapped outside Cardinal's house. Reception at house. Later left for New York on one o'clock [rest of sentence incomplete].

Stopped at Hotel Belmont. Had luncheon at Claridge's. Went to ride in Arthur Goldsmith's machine. Later dined with him at [rest of sentence incomplete].

Went to see Douglas Fairbanks in *He Comes Up Smiling*. Father and John arrive on way to World Series games [Boston Braves vs. Philadelphia Athletics].

Left on Friday morning for Philadelphia where we met all the Royal Rooters led by Father. Took in the game in the afternoon and waited for the second game on Saturday. Taking the train for White Sulphur Springs in the evening. We arrived Sunday morning October eleventh. There we met some delightful as well as distinguished people including Mr. John Hays Hammond, Mr. and Mrs. George Watters, Mr. and Mrs. Clarence Hellman of Louisville and many others. Dr. Kanlo, who had charge of the 'kur,' was most interesting, as well as reliable.

We rode every day, and also enjoyed the tennis and golf. One of the most pleasant evenings was that spent with Mr. and Mrs. Watters where we dined with them.

We left White Sulphur on Wednesday October twenty-second in the evening and reached Atlantic City Thursday afternoon. After trying the bathing we went to the theatre to see Nazimova in a new play which was not especially good. The next morning we promenaded on the board walk and 'had our picture took.' In the afternoon we went back to New York and went to the theatre to see *On Trial*.

Saturday we went to see Montgomery and Stone in *Chin Chin*, later supped and danced at the Biltmore. We returned home Sunday and went to live at Beals Street Wednesday October twenty-eighth."

TRANSCRIPTION FROM ROSE'S "THE WEDDING LOG"

Rose Fitzgerald Kennedy on her wedding day, October 7, 1914.

Rose and Joe's first home, located at 83 Beals Street in
Brookline, Massachusetts.

"It was a nice old wooden-frame house with clapboard siding; seven rooms,
plus two small ones in the converted attic, all on a small lot with a few bushes
and trees. It would have blended perfectly into most of the main streets of Amer-
ica. It was in the Boston suburb of Brookline, yet only about twenty-five minutes
from the center of the city by trolley, the usual means of transportation in those
days. There was a sense of openness in the neighborhood, with a vacant lot on
one side of us and another across the street, and fine big shade trees lining the
sidewalks."

ROSE'S DESCRIPTION OF 83 BEALS STREET,
THE KENNEDYS' FIRST HOME

Rose and Joe ice-skating in Poland Springs, Maine,
February 22, 1915.

❝ We had been going there [Poland Springs] for some years, beginning about
1916, and enjoyed ourselves thoroughly. Sleighs met us at the railroad station and
we were bundled into raccoon coats, with blankets over our legs, and taken to the
hotel with bells jingling and steel runners crunching in the snow. We reveled in
the adventures of skiing the gentle slopes and coasting on the snow and skating
on the ice rink. ❞

ROSE'S DESCRIPTION OF WINTER VACATIONS
IN POLAND SPRINGS, MAINE

Joseph Patrick Kennedy Jr., circa January 1916.

Joe Jr. with his maternal grandfather, Honey Fitz, at Nantasket Beach in Hull, Massachusetts, circa 1916.

Joe and Joe Jr. in Hull, Massachusetts, where the Kennedys were spending the summer, circa 1916.

Joe jr + mother

Rose and Joe Jr. go sledding, circa 1916–1917.

"When a mother holds her first baby in her arms, what awe-inspiring thoughts go fleeting through her mind and fill her heart. A child has been bestowed upon her to mold and to influence—what a challenge, what a joy! From her he will be told, in childish language first and later in firm, uncompromising precepts, what he may do and what is forbidden. On her judgment he relies, and her words will influence him, not for a day or a month or a year, but for time and for eternity— and perhaps for future generations. A grandmother, an aunt, a teacher may guide the child temporarily, but when the mother enters the room, it is to her he turns for the final judgment.

A mother knows that hers is the influence which can make that little, precious being into a leader, an inspiration, a shining light to the world.

What a challenging thought and what an exciting experience for a woman. No award from church or state or university, no accomplishment in business or finance, no fame in the theater or the screen equals that knowledge."

ROSE'S OBSERVATION ON BEING A MOTHER

Rose and Joe Jr., circa 1917.

Joe and Joe Jr. in the backyard of the 83 Beals Street home
in Brookline, Massachusetts, circa 1916–1917.

Three generations of Kennedys: Joe, Joe Jr., and P.J.
at Nantasket Beach, circa 1916–1917.

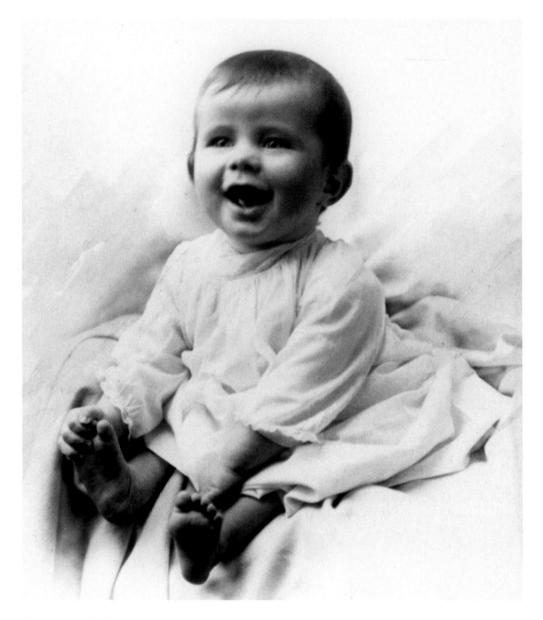

John Fitzgerald Kennedy, circa November 1917.

(OPPOSITE, CLOCKWISE FROM TOP LEFT)

Joe with his two sons, Joe Jr. (left) and Jack, at Nantasket
Beach, circa 1918.

Rosemary, Jack, and Joe Jr. at Nantasket Beach, circa 1919.

Jack and Joe Jr. at Nantasket Beach, circa 1918.

(ABOVE) Joe, Jack, and Joe Jr. in Brookline, circa 1919.

(OPPOSITE) Jack and Joe Jr. dressed in their Sunday best
in Brookline, circa 1919.

(ABOVE) Rosemary, Jack, and Joe Jr. at Nantasket Beach, circa 1921.

(RIGHT) P.J. and Joe with Rosemary (left) and Kathleen at Nantasket Beach, circa 1921.

(ABOVE) Rose with daughters Eunice
and Rosemary at Nantasket Beach, 1922.

(LEFT) Eunice at Nantasket Beach,
on the occasion of her first birthday,
July 1922.

Rose with her five children, circa 1923.
Left to right: Eunice, Rosemary (in forefront),
Kathleen, Jack, and Joe Jr.

Joe and his daughters, Eunice, Rosemary, and
Kathleen, outside their home at 131 Naples Road in
Brookline, circa 1923.

(ABOVE) Joe with his children at Sandy Beach in
Cohasset, Massachusetts, circa 1923–1924.
Left to right: Jack, Rosemary, Kathleen, and Eunice.

(OPPOSITE, TOP) The Kennedy children at Sandy Beach,
circa 1923–1924. Left to right: Eunice, Jack, Joe Jr.,
Rosemary, and Kathleen.

(OPPOSITE, BOTTOM) Rosemary and Jack at Sandy Beach,
circa 1923–1924.

Eunice and Rosemary in Cohasset, circa 1923–1924.

P.J. with Jack and Rosemary in Cohasset, circa 1923–1924.

An early Kennedy lineup in Cohasset, circa 1923–1924.
Top to bottom: Joe Jr., Jack, Rosemary, Kathleen, and
Eunice.

Joe Jr., Kathleen, Rosemary, and Jack on the front steps of
their rented summer house in Cohasset, circa 1923–1924.

(ABOVE) The Kennedy children in Cohasset, circa 1923–1924. Left to right: Kathleen, Rosemary, Eunice, Joe Jr., and Jack.

(RIGHT) Rosemary riding her tricycle in Cohasset, circa 1923–1924.

Eunice, Rosemary, Jack, Joe Jr., and Kathleen in Cohasset,
circa 1923–1924.

Joe Jr., Jack, and Eunice in Brookline, circa 1923–1924.

Jack poses in his police costume while younger sister
Eunice looks on in Brookline, circa 1923–1924.

Jack on skis in Poland Springs, Maine, circa 1923–1924.

Jack (center) and Joe Jr. (right) go sledding with an
unidentified friend in Brookline, circa 1923–1924.

❝ Dear Mother

    we are having a very nice time we go skiing we go sliding and we go to bed the
same time that we go at home and we have a very nice time and we go out avry day
and the horse are good. and one of the horse are lazy and is name is Happy he can
run if he wants to. but hees a good horse just a same. love frome

Jack ❞

LETTER TO HIS MOTHER FROM JACK, MANSION HOUSE,
SOUTH POLAND, MAINE, DECEMBER 29, 1924

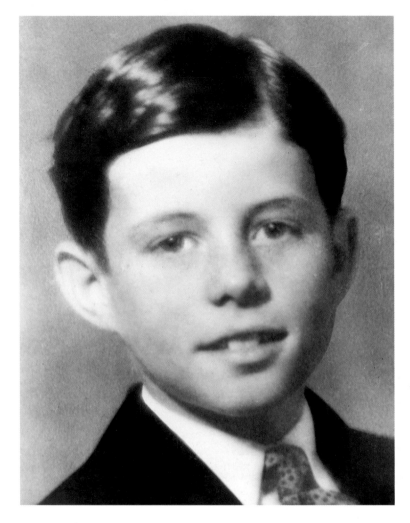

An early school photograph of Jack, circa 1925.

"He had a rather narrow face and his ears stuck out a little bit and his hair wouldn't stay put, and all that added, I suppose, to an elfin quality in his appearance. But he was a very active, very lively elf, full of energy when he wasn't ill and full of charm and imagination. And surprises—for he thought his own thoughts, did things his own way, and somehow just didn't fit any pattern. Now and then, fairly often in fact, that distressed me, since I thought I knew what was best. But at the same time that I was taken aback, I was enchanted and amused. He was a funny little boy, and he said things in such an original, vivid way…"

ROSE'S DESCRIPTION OF JACK AS A YOUNG BOY

Jack on the occasion of his First Communion, Brookline, June 1925.

The Kennedy's sixth child and fourth daughter, Patricia Kennedy, in Brookline, circa 1925.

Eunice, Kathleen, and Rosemary in Brookline, circa 1925.

Joe Jr. and Jack in Hyannis Port, Massachusetts,
circa 1925.

"…during the earlier years of their boyhood there were fights, few of which I
saw but some of which I have been told were real battles. Joe, Jr. was older, bigger,
stronger, but Jack, frail though he was, could fight like fury when he had to. He
had wonderful physical coordination. Thankfully, they probably fought no more
than other brothers so close in age do and, in fact, possibly less. "

ROSE'S DESCRIPTION OF THE RELATIONSHIP
BETWEEN JOE JR. AND JACK

(CLOCKWISE, FROM LEFT)

Jack and the family dog, circa 1925–1926.

Kathleen (left) and Rosemary pose with Jack, who is proudly holding his trophy, circa 1925.

Joe and Eunice at Craigville Beach in Centerville, Massachusetts, circa 1925.

“ Mother and I congratulate Jack on his fine swim Also Rosemary and Kathleen Next year Eunice will win We are having wonderful weather and a fine time Expect to leave for Biarritz on Tuesday Will cable you my address there Glad to hear everybody is well and hope you are all enjoying yourselves Love from Mother and Daddy

Kennedy ”

TELEGRAM FROM JOSEPH P. KENNEDY SR. TO
FAMILY FRIEND EDWARD MOORE, AUGUST 28, 1926

Joe Jr. holding Bobby, Jack, Rosemary, Kathleen, Eunice, and Pat, circa 1926.

Rose, Pat, and Kathleen, circa 1926.

"…in my family there weren't a great many opportunities to be with Grandpa all by myself. There was always a crowd of kids and adults wanting to spend time with him. However, there were a few special occasions when he did things that didn't draw a following. He liked to go to the ocean and sit in the seaweed.

My mother always wanted to ensure that there was someone with him when he undertook this adventure so, at the age of 13 or 14, I would often accompany Grandpa to the water's edge while he performed this ritual. Grandpa would tell me it was good for his health to do this. So I would sit and watch and wait till he was finished. We wouldn't talk much together, but I would listen to what he had to say and what he had on his mind at the time. "

EUNICE DESCRIBING TIME SPENT WITH
HER GRANDFATHER FITZGERALD

Honey Fitz and Pat on the beach, circa 1926.

The Dexter School football team in Brookline, 1926. Jack is seated on the ground to the far right, and Joe Jr. is third to the left in the first row.

CLASS OF SERVICE	SYMBOL
TELEGRAM	
DAY LETTER	BLUE
NIGHT MESSAGE	NITE
NIGHT LETTER	N L

If none of these three symbols appears after the check (number of words) this is a telegram. Otherwise its character is indicated by the symbol appearing after the check.

WESTERN UNION
TELEGRAM

NEWCOMB CARLTON, PRESIDENT   J. C. WILLEVER, FIRST VICE-PRESIDENT

CLASS OF SERVICE	SYMBOL
TELEGRAM	
DAY LETTER	BLUE
NIGHT MESSAGE	NITE
NIGHT LETTER	N L

If none of these three symbols appears after the check (number of words) this is a telegram. Otherwise its character is indicated by the symbol appearing after the check.

The filing time as shown in the date line on full-rate telegrams and day letters, and the time of receipt at destination as shown on all messages, is STANDARD TIME.

Received at 169 Congress Street, Boston, Mass.

DUPLICATE OF TELEPHONED TELEGRAM

NB89 20 FI NEWYORK NY 19 842A

1926 MAY 19 AM 8 59

CAPTAIN JACK KENNEDY.

NOBLE AND GREENOUGH LAW SCHOOL PLEASANT ST BROOKLINE MASS

.DEAR JACK GOOD LUCK TO THE TEAM IN YOUR GAME WITH RIVERS

THIS AFTERNOON AND HOPE YOU ALL PLAY WELL.

.DADDY.

Telegram to Jack from his father, May 19, 1926.

HARVARD CLUB
27 WEST 44TH STREET

Rosa dear,

I am getting ready to go now & when you get this I will be on my way, but I will be coming back soon so please don't be too lonesome & have a great time.

I just want you to know that going away

"Rosa dear,

I am getting ready to go now & when you get this I will be on my way, but I will be coming back soon so please don't be too lonesome & have a great time.

I just want you to know that going away on trips like this makes me realize just how little anything amounts to except you. As years go on I just love you more than anything in the world and I always wonder whether I ever do half enough for you to show you how much I appreciate you.

Well dear this is just a little love letter from a husband to wife married 11 years.

Break 50 if you have to take a lesson morning & night.

The "Popper" said today he would be down soon so you'll be busy & I'll be home before you know it.

Love to you & my wonderful family.
Joe "

on trips like this makes me realize just how little anything amounts to except you. As years go on I just love you more than anything in the world and I always wonder whether I ever do half enough for you to show you how much I appreciate you.

Well dear this is just a little love letter

from a husband to wife married 11 years.

Break 50 if you have to take a lesson morning & night.

The "Pepper" said today he would be down soon so you'll be busy & I'll be home before you know it.

Love to you & my wonderful family.

Joe

LETTER FROM JOSEPH P. KENNEDY SR. TO
ROSE KENNEDY, CIRCA 1925

NOTE: Rosa was a term of endearment used by Joseph P. Kennedy Sr.

Rose and Joe on Christmas Day in Bronxville, 1933.

THE BRONXVILLE
YEARS

The 1920s was a roaring decade, sandwiched between the end of World War I and the Great Depression, a decade of frenzied excess tempered by alcohol prohibition, a decade in which industrial capitalism and progressive reform clashed on the world stage. It was a promising time for the Kennedys, with Joe's success in business, the growth of the Kennedy clan, and new prospects for a young family.

Now firmly established in the motion picture business, Joe decided to move the family closer to his offices in New York. On September 26, 1927, the Kennedy family boarded a private railroad car for their new home in Riverdale, an affluent neighborhood in the northwest Bronx, New York, located on 252nd Street and Independence Avenue. The Kennedy family settled into a rented house with a view of the Hudson River and surrounded by woods. Later, in 1929, Joe purchased a five-acre estate in Bronxville, Westchester County, New York, known as the "Crownlands." The Georgian-style house had twenty rooms spread out on three floors. Separate residential quarters were also available for a chauffeur and a gardener.

Joe Sr. was gaining enormous success in Hollywood. His achievements with FBO had been noticed, and he was invited to perform similar corporate turnarounds, first for Pathé-DeMille and then with First National. As a condition of his work, Joe requested absolute power in these companies, and in fact wound up in control of Pathé. But the requirement did not sit well with the board of First National, which ultimately dispensed with his services. Still, for a brief period of time in 1928, Joe was the de facto head of four different companies.

Although the Kennedy family was now settled in New York, Joe and Rose maintained their ties to the Boston area. Starting in 1925, the Kennedys began vacationing in Hyannis Port on Cape Cod, at a rented summer home, locally referred to as Malcolm Cottage, on Marchant Avenue. The Kennedys loved the area so much that Joe purchased Malcolm Cottage from Beulah Malcolm in November 1928. Erected in 1904, the original structure of the house was enlarged and remodeled over the years to fit the growing needs of the family. It was here at Hyannis Port that the Kennedy children acquired their life-long interest in sailing.

Rose was pregnant when the family moved to Riverdale, and it was her wish that all the children be born in Massachusetts and delivered by the same physician, Dr. Frederick Good. So, in 1928, she traveled back to Boston, where Jean Ann was born on February 20 at St. Margaret's Hospital and was later baptized at the Kennedys' former neighborhood church, St. Aidan's Catholic Church in Brookline. Four years later, Rose returned to St. Margaret's

(BOTTOM, LEFT) Jean, Bobby, Pat, and Eunice dressed in costume for Halloween in Bronxville, 1932.

(BOTTOM, RIGHT) Eunice, Kikoo (Katherine Conboy) holding Teddy, Jean, and Bobby in Bronxville, New York, May 1932.

Hospital to deliver Edward Moore on February 22, 1932.

At first, the older Kennedy children attended the Riverdale Country School. Joe, who had high expectations for his sons, sent Joe Jr. to the Choate School, a private boarding school in Wallingford, Connecticut, after he graduated from Riverdale. Jack spent an academic year at the Canterbury School in New Milford, Connecticut, in 1930–1931. The year was not a promising one for Jack, who was plagued by ill health and poor grades, and his father withdrew him from Canterbury and enrolled him at Choate, where Joe Jr. had had a very successful academic year. Rose wanted Kick to have a religious education and enrolled her at the Sacred Heart Convent in Noroton, Connecticut.

Joe Jr.'s success at Choate culminated in 1933, his final year there, when he won the coveted Harvard Football Trophy, which is "awarded annually to that member of the football squad who best combines scholarship and sportsmanship." After spending a year at the London School of Economics studying with Professor Harold Laski, Joe Jr. entered Harvard College in the fall of 1934.

Though Jack was not the best student, his Choate headmaster noted that he had a "clever, individualist mind." He did not always work as hard as he could, except in his favorite subjects, history and English. This appears to have been Jack's particular study habit since childhood. In 1923, Rose noted in her diary that Jack, in relating to her the news that his teacher was coming to the house to "tell on him," stated: "You know I am getting on all right and if you study too much, you're liable to go crazy." Jack performed well enough to graduate from Choate in the spring of 1935.

Beginning in the mid-1930s, the older Kennedy children would begin to travel extensively throughout Europe. In September 1935, Jack and Kick embarked on their first European voyage with their

parents. Like his older brother, Jack was to spend the next year studying at the London School of Economics. Since Jack would be nearby in London and knowing of the close relationship he shared with Kick, Rose thought Kick should spend a year at the Holy Child Convent in Neuilly, France.

Although a sudden illness forced Jack to return to the United States shortly after his arrival in England, Kick continued her studies in France for the following year, with occasional trips to Switzerland and Italy. She would particularly enjoy a memorable trip to Moscow with Rose in the spring of 1936. Jack, meanwhile, recovered from his illness and enrolled at Princeton University for the 1935 fall semester, where he roomed with Choate friends Rip Horton and Lem Billings. But once again Jack's health declined, compelling him to leave Princeton and spend the remainder of 1935 and early 1936 recuperating at the family's Palm Beach estate and the Jay-6 Ranch in Arizona. Following in the footsteps

of his father and older brother, Jack then enrolled at Harvard College in the fall of 1936.

Eunice followed Kick to the Sacred Heart Convent in Connecticut while Pat, who was younger than Eunice by three years, remained in Bronxville and attended the Maplehurst Sacred Heart Convent School.

Eunice and Rosemary traveled to Switzerland in 1936, accompanied by their governess, Elizabeth Dunn. In 1937 Joe Jr., Kick, and Rose traveled to Ireland and then England, where they would meet up with Jack, who had been touring Europe with close friend Lem Billings.

When the stock market crash of 1929 launched the decade-long Great Depression, Joe had already cashed out his fortune. Joe's foray into Hollywood had brought him a large and significantly liquid fortune that allowed him to invest in real estate. In addition to buying the summer house in Hyannis Port, he purchased a winter home in Palm Beach, Florida, in 1933, well before Florida became a popular vacation destination. Joe bought the Addison Mizner–designed house for $120,000 from the family of retailer Rodman Wanamaker on June 30, 1933. Located at 1095 North Ocean Boulevard, the relatively new (ten-year-old) house consisted of 11 rooms on 1.6 acres.

At the beginning of the 1930s, the real focus of Joe's energies shifted to politics. Although he came from a solidly Democratic pedigree, Joe had wavered from that allegiance and at one point had

(OPPOSITE, LEFT) Eunice, Bobby, Joe Jr., Jack holding Jean, Rosemary, and Pat (sitting) in Hyannis Port, circa 1933.

(OPPOSITE, RIGHT) Pat, Rose, and Bobby on the occasion of Pat and Bobby's First Communion, April 30, 1933.

(RIGHT) A photograph of the Palm Beach estate as it appeared in March 1934.

considered joining the Republican Party. But the Great Depression had shaken his faith in Republican solutions. Believing a change was necessary to preserve the system, and willing to accept the toll on his own wealth that might be involved, Joe threw his personal and financial support behind Franklin Delano Roosevelt in the 1932 presidential campaign. Using his connections on Wall Street and in Hollywood, Joe helped raise significant money for the campaign, helping to ensure Roosevelt's victory.

Joe's support of Roosevelt whetted his political ambitions, and so he was initially disappointed when Roosevelt did not immediately find a place for him in his new administration. Finally, in July 1934, Roosevelt appointed him chairman of the newly created Securities and Exchange Commission (SEC). Joe's tenure as the first chairman of the SEC proved to be a success. Though he had been appointed for a five-year term, Joe resigned from the SEC in September 1935, believing he had accomplished his mission, which was to establish the new Commission in its first year and to set up policy guidelines to prevent Wall Street excesses and to protect investors in the future.

During the next year Joe acted as a consultant in business and government. After a six-week tour of Europe in the fall of 1935, he reported to Roosevelt on the European economic situation. He followed up that work with a more formalized stint as a paid advisor to David Sarnoff of RCA, which had

suffered dangerous setbacks in the early Depression years. Joe also briefly returned to the movie industry, preparing a business review at the request of Paramount Pictures.

The 1936 presidential campaign brought Joe back into politics. Roosevelt again sought his help on the campaign, and Kennedy responded with his book, *I'm for Roosevelt*. Written with the help of his friend *New York Times* columnist Arthur Krock, the book, told from Joe's personal perspective, offered arguments for why businessmen should support Roosevelt and his New Deal platform, which sought to counter the Great Depression through government reform and a jobs program for the unemployed. The book had a significant impact in the business community, and after his reelection, Roosevelt appointed Joe chairman of the United States Maritime Commission. Created by the Merchant Marine Act of 1936, the Commission was expected to rejuvenate America's merchant shipping industry, which was crippled by an outdated fleet and a difficult labor situation. Joe would spend ten months at the Commission.

In early December 1937, Roosevelt named Kennedy as the new ambassador to the Court of St. James, the United States' representative to Great Britain and the first Irish Catholic ever to be appointed to the position. Joe officially resigned from the Maritime Commission in February 1938 and prepared to take up residence at 14 Prince's Gate in London.

Joe Jr. on the occasion of his
Confirmation in Brookline,
Massachusetts, May 14, 1927.

131 Naples Road Brookline May 15, 1927

" Dearest Mother,

I thank you and dad for the lovely telegram. The most important thing I have to tell you is that I was confirmed yesterday by Cardinal O'conell. I served and received Holy Communion at seven o'clock mass, then I came home and had breakfast, changed my clothes and was back at the hall at nine. About ten o'clock we started for the church in a prosession. Confirmation was a ten thirty prompt. Eddy, Mrs. Moore, Rose, and Ennice Aunt Loretta, grandpa and grandma Fitzgerald and Aunt Agnes were there. Grandpa Kennedy had to go to a funeral (Dr. Gibline) The church was pretty well crowded.

The services were over at quarter past eleven and then we had our picture taken. Then I went home and changed my clothes and went out to Billy Butler's.

I thank you very much for the prayer book you gave me. Grandpa Kennedy gave me a five dollar gold piece and Aunt Agnes and grandma gave me some rosary beads, Grandpa Fitzgearld gave me a signet ring. I went out to Billy Butlers who was having a party and then went with him to the movies.

The weather has been rainy and chilly every day since you left. Kathleen is going to receive her first communion next Sunday. I hope you are feeling well every body around here is feeling good. I will have to close now with best love to you and daddy

Your Loving Son,
Joe "

LETTER FROM JOE JR. TO HIS MOTHER, MAY 15, 1927

The Kennedy children at the hippodrome: Jack (center),
Joe Jr., Kathleen, Eunice, and Rosemary (far right),
December 1927.

The Kennedy family Christmas card, 1927.

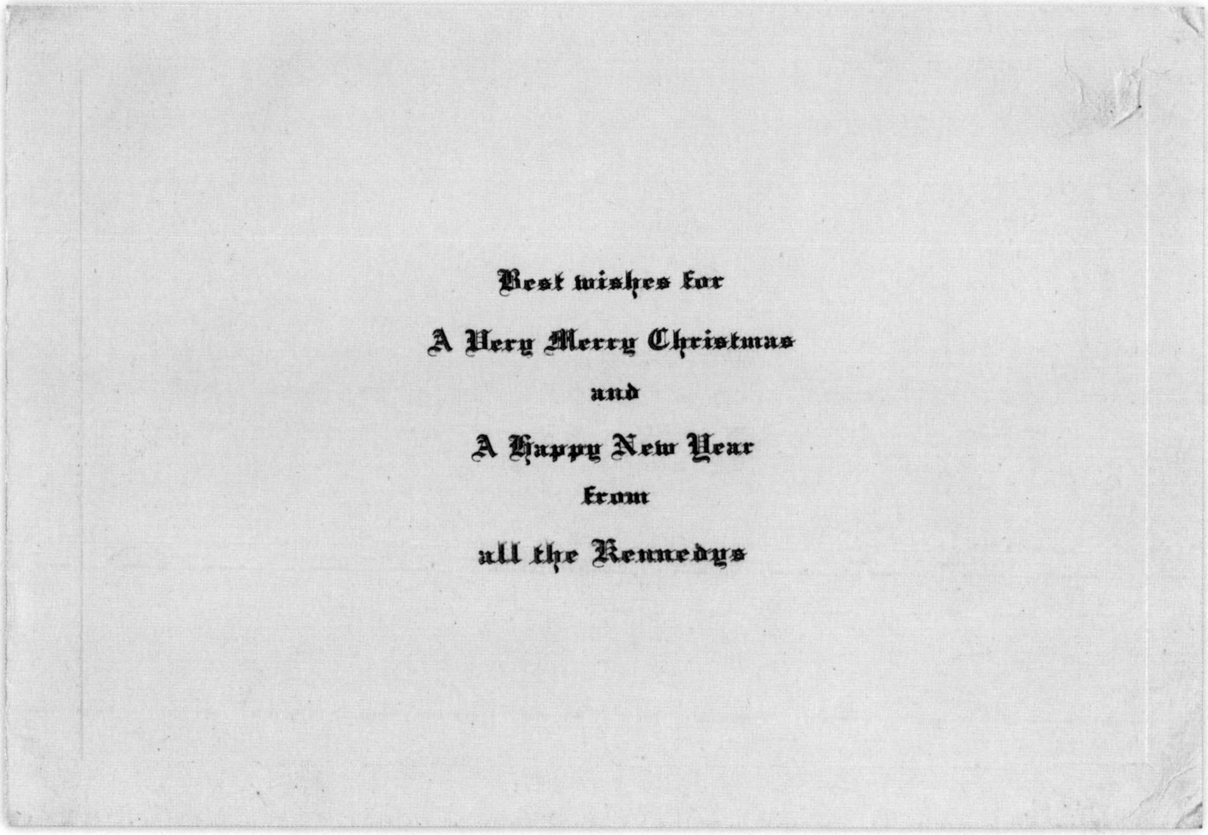

Best wishes for

A Very Merry Christmas

and

A Happy New Year

from

all the Kennedys

(ABOVE) Jean, Rose, and Bobby in Hyannis Port,
circa 1928.

(OPPOSITE) Rosemary and Jack on the day of their
Confirmation, Riverdale, New York, April 27, 1928.

Jean, Bobby, Pat, Eunice, Kathleen, Rosemary, Jack, and Joe Jr. in Hyannis Port, circa August 1928.

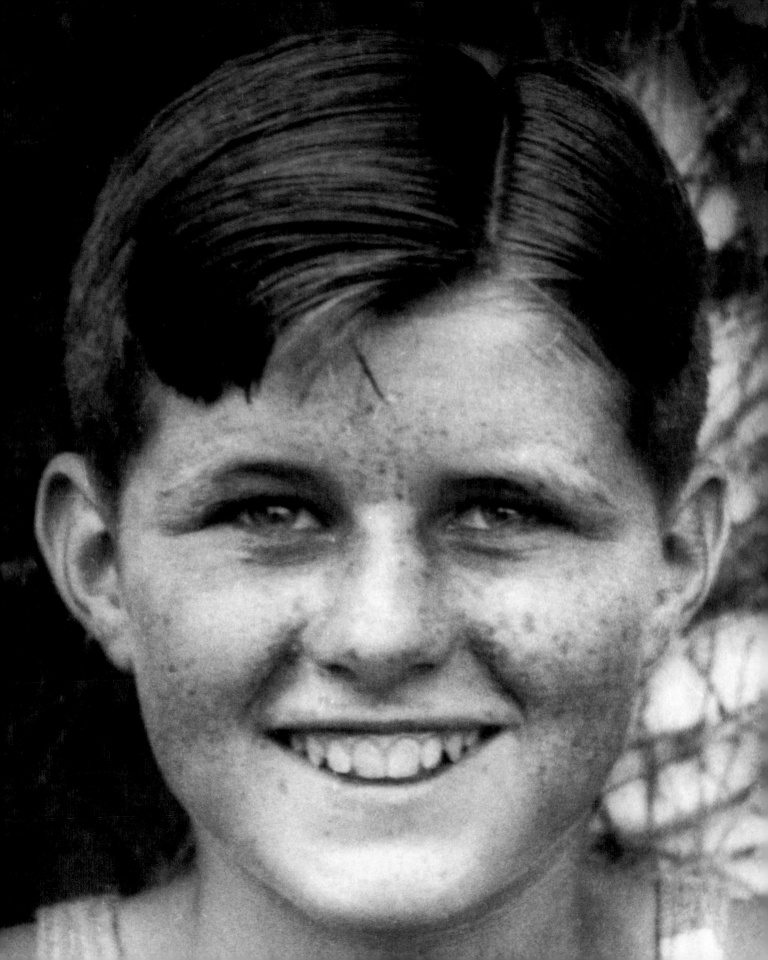

(OPPOSITE) Joe Jr. in Hyannis Port, circa August 1928.

(BELOW) Pat in Hyannis Port, circa August 1928.

(ABOVE) Bobby, P.J., and Pat in Hyannis Port, circa 1928.

(LEFT) Jean and Joe in Hyannis Port, circa 1930.

(RIGHT) The Kennedy children line up in the water with Rose leading the way: Bobby, Pat, Eunice, Kathleen (hidden behind Eunice), Rosemary, Jack, and Joe Jr., circa 1928.

Pat, Eunice, Kathleen, and Rosemary
play dress-up in Hyannis Port,
circa 1928.

(ABOVE) Pat, Kathleen, Eunice, and Rosemary on the occasion of Eunice's First Communion, Bronxville, New York, circa 1929.

(OPPOSITE, TOP) Rosemary, Pat, Kathleen, and Eunice in Riverdale, New York, circa 1928.

(OPPOSITE, BOTTOM) Bobby and Pat on the double swing in Riverdale, circa 1928.

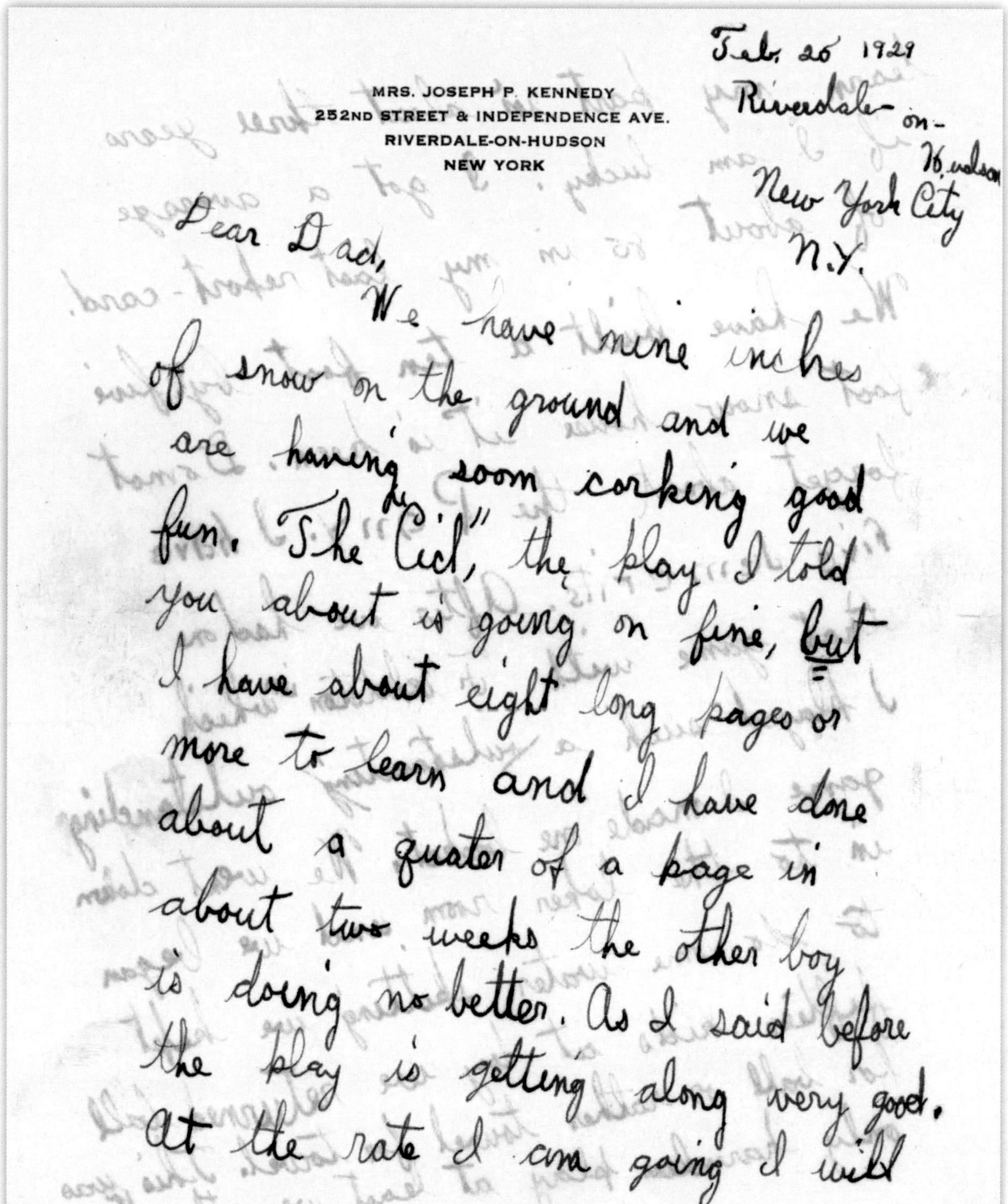

MRS. JOSEPH P. KENNEDY
252ND STREET & INDEPENDENCE AVE.
RIVERDALE-ON-HUDSON
NEW YORK

Feb, 25 1929
Riverdale- on-
Hudson
New York City
N.Y.

Dear Dad,
We have nine inches of snow on the ground and we are having some corking good fun. "The Ciel," the play I told you about is going on fine, but I have about eight long pages or more to learn and I have done about a quater of a page in about two weeks the other boy is doing no better. As I said before the play is getting along very good. At the rate I am going I will

(ABOVE) Letter from Jack to his father, February 25, 1929.

(OPPOSITE) John F. Kennedy, circa 1932–1933.

(CONTINUED)

learn my part in about three years
if I am lucky. I got a average
of about 85 in my last report-card.
We have built a ten foot by five
foot snow house it is keen. Do not
forget about the Pony. I have
five demerits. After we had one
that game with fieldston in which
I played such a outstanding
game I made one basket. We went down
in to the loker room and we began
to do some water skitting we kept
fifteen kids at bay we returned ball
for ball or rather towel for towel. This was
only harmless play at least we thought

MRS. JOSEPH P. KENNEDY
252ND STREET & INDEPENDENCE AVE.
RIVERDALE-ON-HUDSON
NEW YORK

it was. Then the teacher came in and
we _ _ _ _ _ _ _ _ _ _ _ _, I have just
had my eyes examined but I do not have to
have glasses. I wish you were home.

Your loving son

Jack Kennedy

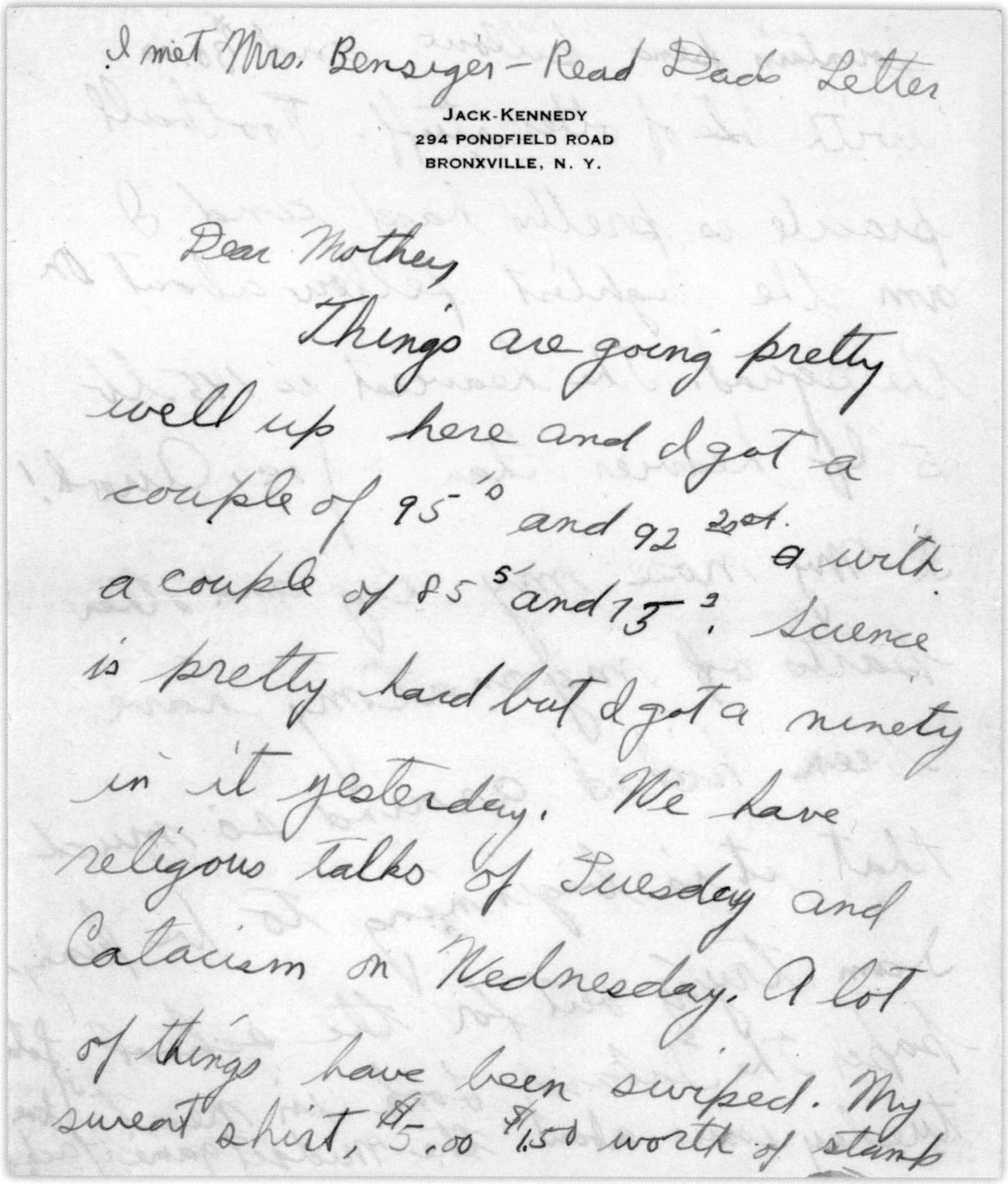

I met Mrs. Bensiger – Read Dads Letter

JACK·KENNEDY
294 PONDFIELD ROAD
BRONXVILLE, N. Y.

Dear Mother,

Things are going pretty well up here and I got a couple of 95 ⁰ and 92 ^{2nd}. a with a couple of 85 ⁵ and 15 ². Science is pretty hard but I got a ninety in it yesterday. We have religious talks of Tuesday and Catacism on Wednesday. A lot of things have been swiped. My sweat shirt, $5.00 $1.50 worth of stamp

Letter from Jack to Rose during his time boarding at the Canterbury School in New Milford, Connecticut, circa 1930–1931.

fountain pens pillows and $30.00 with lots of other stuff. Football pracite is pretty hard and I am the lightest fellow about on the squad. The heaviest is 145 lb 5 lb heavier than Joe. Awok! My nose my leg and other parts of my anatomy have been kicked around so much that it is beginning to be funny. I am trying out for the school paper The Tabard. Look in next tuesday issue about the Midget game

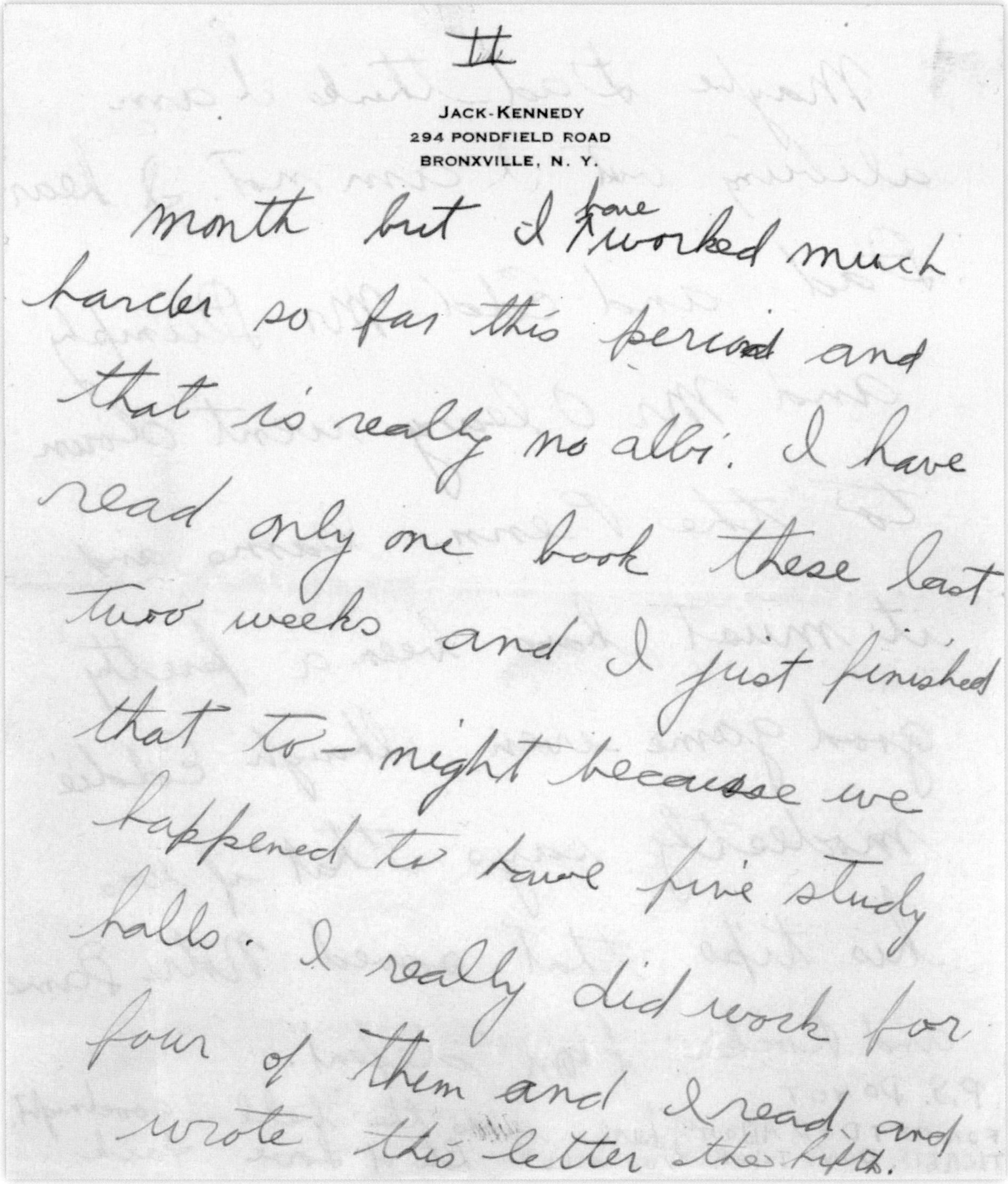

JACK·KENNEDY
294 PONDFIELD ROAD
BRONXVILLE, N. Y.

month but I have worked much harder so far this period and that is really no alibi. I have read only one book these last two weeks and I just finished that to-night because we happened to have five study halls. I really did work for four of them and I read and wrote this letter the fifth.

An excerpt of a letter from Jack to his mother,
circa November 1930.

Maybe Dad thinks I am
alibiing but I am not. I hear
Dad and Edd Mr Dumphy
and Mr O'Leary went down
to the Penn. Game and
it must have been a pretty
good game even though Eddie
modestly says that if was
his tips that saved Notre Dame
and Rockne from defeat.

P.S. DO NOT
FOR GET DAD ABOUT There goes the bell — goodnight.
TICKETS. DON'T THINK YOU WILL Lots of Love Jack

121

Joe Jr., Joe, and Jack in Palm Beach, Florida, circa 1930.

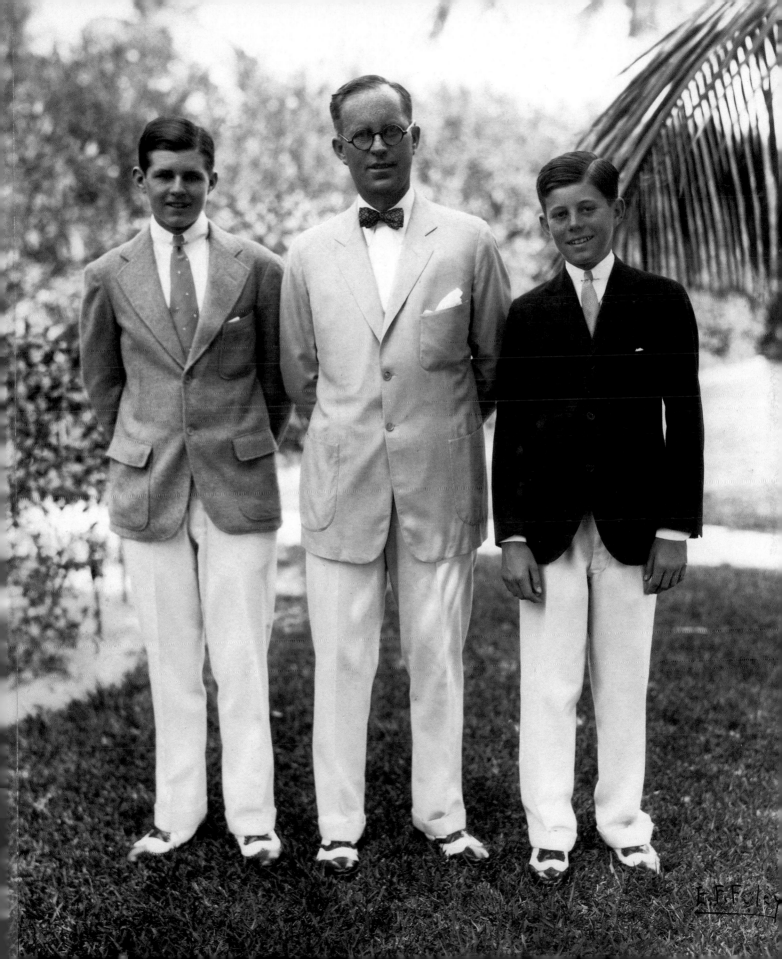

Rosemary on horseback, circa 1930–1931.

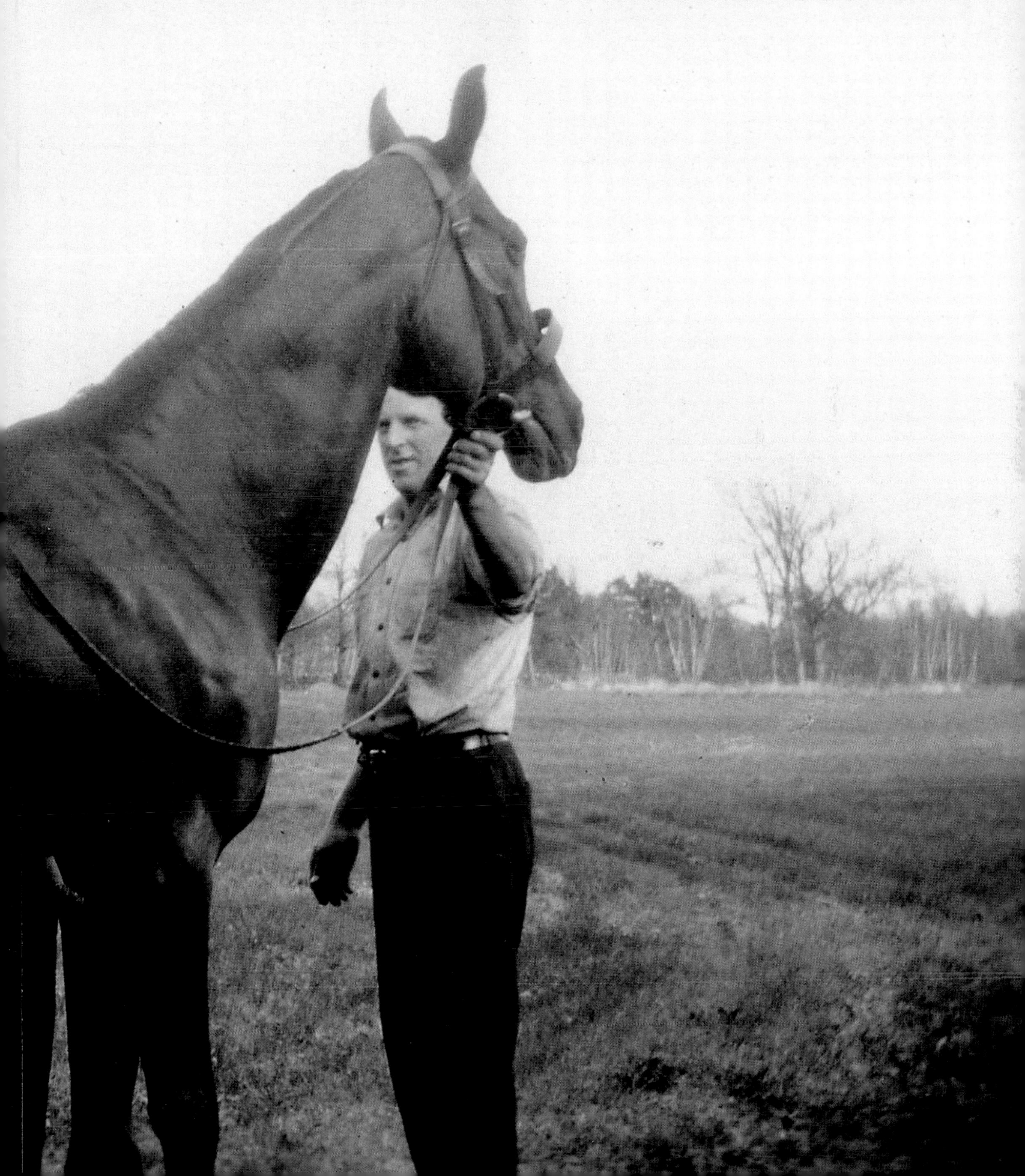

PHOTO BY
RICHARD W. SEARS, BOSTON

A PLEA FOR A RAISE
BY JACK KENNEDY
DEDICATED TO MY MR. J.P. KENNEDY
CHAPTER I

"My recent allowance is 40¢. This I used for areoplanes and other playthings of childhood but now I am a scout and I put away my childish things. Before I would spend 20¢ of my ¢40 allowance and in five minutes I would have empty pockets and nothing to gain and 20¢ to lose. When I am a scout I have to buy canteens, haversacks, blankets, searchlidgs, poncho things that will last for years and I can always use it while I can't use a cholcalote marshmellow sunday with vanilla ice cream and so I put in my plea for a raise of thirty cents for me to buy scout things and pay my own way more around."

LETTER FROM JACK TO HIS FATHER
ASKING FOR AN INCREASE IN HIS ALLOWANCE

(ABOVE) Joe Jr., Jack, Rosemary, Kathleen, Eunice, Pat, Bobby, and Jean in Hyannis Port, September 4, 1931.

(OPPOSITE) Bobby takes Jean out on his skiff, the *Bobby*, in Hyannis Port, September 4, 1931.

Rosemary in Hyannis Port, September 4, 1931.

Eunice in Hyannis Port, September 4, 1931.

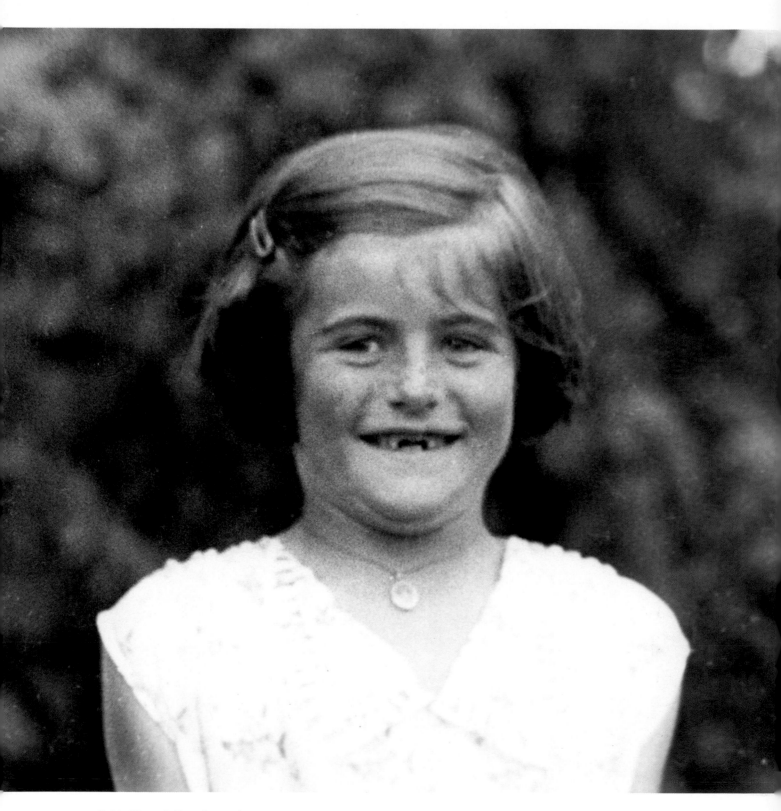

Pat in Hyannis Port, September 4, 1931.

Jean in Hyannis Port, September 4, 1931.

Bobby, Jack, Eunice, Jean, Joe, Rose, Pat (in front of Rose),
Kathleen, Joe Jr., and Rosemary on the beach in Hyannis
Port, September 4, 1931.

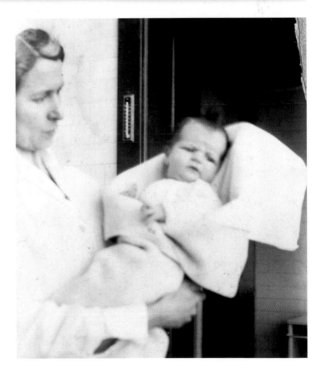

THE CHOATE SCHOOL
WALLINGFORD, CONNECTICUT

Dear Mother,

It is the night before exams so I will write you Wednesday.

Lots of Love.

P.S. Can I be Godfather to the baby*

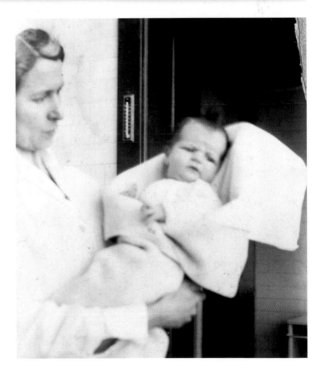

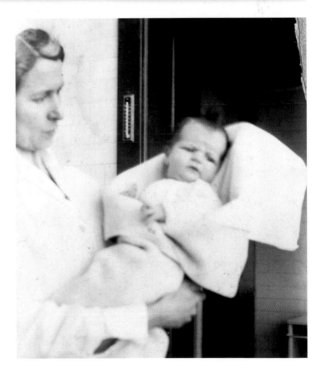

(ABOVE) An undated letter from Jack to his mother, Rose, circa February 1932, asking to be Teddy's godfather.

(RIGHT) Edward Moore Kennedy, five days after his birth at St. Margaret's Hospital in Boston, Massachusetts, February 27, 1932.

(OPPOSITE) Jack in Palm Beach, Florida, circa 1931.

135

Jack (second to the right) and his fellow teammates at the
Choate School in Wallingford, Connecticut, circa 1932–1933.

Teddy at ten months in Bronxville,
December 1932.

Bronxville, New York
December 1932

" Dear Jack,

I am sending you the reports which were with some of Daddy's things. I hope you will keep up the good work—even if you think sometimes it is foolish. As I said before, your Latin helps you to spell and talk correctly, and other things such as Geometry help you to reason, etc., so learn them well whether you like them or not.

The little girls are fine and roller skating again. Ted is standing up at his crib and has a couple of teeth.

I guess this is about all the news. Are you in danger of breaking your nose in football? If you are—please stop.

Be sure to say your prayers. Put something to remind you, as it is a serious matter.

Much love to you from us all,
Mother "

LETTER TO JACK FROM HIS MOTHER

Joe Jr. in his football uniform at the Choate School,
circa 1933.

Sunday, February 5, 1933

❝Dear Dad & Mother:

...I spent all to-day filling in my applications to Harvard & Dartmouth. You have to give your whole history as well as that of your parents. I put you down as graduating in the class of 1912 and as being born in 1890. Is that right? I don't think it makes much difference as long as you get it approximately. I have some pictures taken of me in football uniform that I will send you this week. I got the oranges. Thanks a lot. That's about all the news.

Love
Joe ❞

EXCERPT OF A LETTER FROM JOE JR. TO HIS PARENTS

Jean and Teddy in Bronxville, April 1933.

Joe Jr., Jack, Rosemary, Kathleen, Eunice, Pat, Bobby, Jean, Teddy, and Rose in front of the Kennedy home in Hyannis Port, circa August 1933.

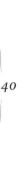

Jack and a classmate goof for the camera as they dance on
the Choate school grounds, circa 1933–1934.

" Jack has done better work as the year has gone on. He still falls down badly on the mechanics of writing; his expression is apt to be vague and wrongly worded. I have disliked his casualness in study which has kept Jack from getting honor grades, but his intelligent interest has made it a pleasure to work with him. "

REPORT FROM THE CHOATE SCHOOL ON JACK'S PERFORMANCE IN
HISTORY CLASS DURING THE FOURTH QUARTER

" I'd like to take the responsibility for Jack's constant lack of neatness about his room and person, since he lived with me for two years. But in the matter of neatness, despite a genuine effort on Jack's part, I must confess to failure.

Occasionally we did manage to effect a house cleaning, but it necessitated my 'dumping' everything in the room into a pile in the middle of the floor. Jack's room has throughout the year been subject to instant and unannounced inspection—it was the only way to maintain a semblance of neatness, for Jack's room was a club for his friends.

I regard the matter of neatness or lack of it on Jack's part as quite symbolic—aside from the value it has in itself—for he is casual and disorderly in almost all of his organization projects. Jack studies at the last minute, keeps appointments late, has little sense of material value, and can seldom locate his possessions.

Despite all this, Jack has had a thoroughly genuine try at being neat according to his own standards and he has been almost religiously on time throughout the Quarter.

I believe Jack began to sense the fitness of things after his midwinter difficulties, and he has and is trying to be a more socially-minded person. "

REPORT FROM THE CHOATE SCHOOL ON JACK'S
NEATNESS AT SCHOOL

Pat, Jean, and Bobby in Bronxville, circa 1933.

(CLOCKWISE, FROM RIGHT)

Bobby demonstrates his skill at skiing in front of the Kennedy home in Bronxville, February 1934.

Bobby, Pat, and Eunice go tobogganing in Bronxville, February 1934.

Family friend Jean Webber and Teddy watch as sister Jean takes her turn on the sled in Bronxville, January 1934.

Teddy on a toboggan in Bronxville, January 1934.

Kathleen prepares to dive into the pool at The Breakers,
Palm Beach, March 1934.

"On my vacation I went to Palm Beach. We went to visit the alligator farm. We saw little and big alligators. We saw monkeys, too. They also had a porcupine. I had a pet rabbit, and we had a pool of our own outside our big house. One day we went fishing. We caught two turtles and no fish. But that was enough, because one turtle weighed 350 pounds and the other 400 pounds. We caught them out at sea. We killed them. This is the end of my story and also the end of the turtles."

Bobby Kennedy

SHORT STORY WRITTEN BY BOBBY FOR THE LAWRENCE PARK WEST COUNTRY DAY SCHOOL NEWSPAPER, DATED APRIL 1934

Lem Billings, Jack, and Bobby sitting on one of the two turtles they caught while fishing in Palm Beach, circa 1934.

Pat and Bobby in Palm Beach, 1934.

Bobby and his rabbit on Easter Sunday
in Palm Beach, April 1, 1934.

Rosemary, Bobby, Pat, Eunice, Joe, Teddy, Rose, and Jean
in Palm Beach, Easter 1934.

Teddy, Jean, Bobby, Pat, Eunice, Kathleen, Rosemary, Jack, Rose, and Joe in Palm Beach, 1934.

(OPPOSITE) Eunice "bests" Kathleen on the tennis court in Palm Beach, circa 1934.

(BELOW) Jean, Eunice, Bobby, and Pat play a game of touch football in Bronxville, October 1934.

(ABOVE) Joe Jr. with the catch of the day
in Hyannis Port, 1934.

(OPPOSITE) Edward E. Moore with his
namesake, Edward Moore Kennedy, in
Hyannis Port, 1934.

The Kennedy family in Hyannis Port, July 1934. Pat, Joe Jr., Bobby, Kathleen, Rose, Jack, Rosemary, Teddy, Joe, Jean, and Eunice.

Joseph P. Kennedy and his sons,
Teddy, Jack, Joe Jr., and Bobby in
Hyannis Port, July 1934.

Jack in profile, circa 1934–1935.

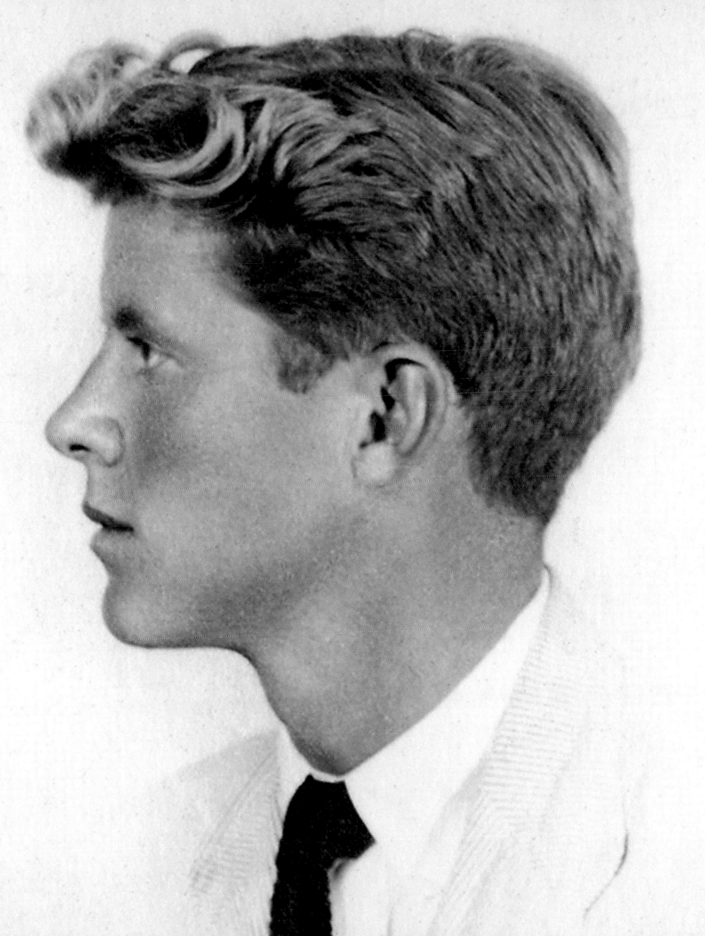

Teddy in Palm Beach, January 1935.

(ABOVE) Joe and Teddy go for a swim at the Palm Beach
estate, March 1935.

(LEFT) Teddy and Eunice in Palm Beach, January 1935.

(ABOVE, AND LEFT) Teddy demonstrates his boxing skills at the Sea Spray Club in Palm Beach, February 1935.

(OPPOSITE) Bobby and Teddy in Palm Beach, circa 1935.

(ABOVE) Kathleen on Easter Sunday in Bronxville, 1935.

(OPPOSITE) Jean in the rock garden of the Bronxville
estate on the day of her First Communion, spring 1935.

(ABOVE) Joe Jr. in Palm Beach, circa February 1935.

(OPPOSITE) Jack and Rosemary in Hyannis Port, circa 1935.

Rosemary reading on the beach in Hyannis Port,
circa 1935.

Jack, Joe, Rose, and Kathleen aboard the SS *Normandie*,
September 25, 1935.

(CLOCKWISE, FROM LEFT)

Bobby at play in Bronxville, October 1935.

Teddy enjoys an outdoor picnic on the Bronxville estate, circa 1935.

Jean and Teddy in Bronxville, circa 1935.

Jean, Pat, Bobby, and Teddy in the backyard of the Kennedy home in Bronxville with the pet rabbits Bobby raises and sells, October 1935.

Bobby in Bronxville, December 1935.

Eunice and Pat go skiing in Bronxville, December 1935.

We're puttin' on our top hat,
Tyin' up our white tie,
Brushin' off our tails,

In order to
Wish you

A Merry Christmas

Rip.   Leem.   Ken.

(ABOVE) Bill Coleman, Jack, and Zeke Coleman in Palm
Beach, circa 1935–1936.

(OPPOSITE) A 1935 Christmas card from three Princeton
University roommates: Rip [Ralph Horton], Leem [Lem
Billings], and Ken [Jack Kennedy].

(ABOVE) Teddy, Pat, Eunice, Jean, Bobby, and Joe Jr. in
Bronxville, February 1936.

(OPPOSITE) Teddy rides a pony, January 1936.

Joe Jr. holding two puppies at the Jay-6 Ranch, Arizona, circa 1936. The original notation that appeared on this photograph was: "Said to be Kathleen Kennedy's favorite photograph of JPK Jr."

(LEFT) Eunice aboard the *Queen Mary*, August 10, 1936.

(OPPOSITE) Eunice and Rosemary on the steamer *Geneve*, on Lake Geneva sailing from Geneva to Montreux, Switzerland, July 12, 1936.

Mon. July 13

" Dear Mother and Dad,

Left Paris Saturday for Geneva. Enjoyed Geneva very much and the scenery was beautiful. Saw where the league of nations met, and a few other places. Left for Montreaux Sunday by steamer and the scenery was the most beautiful I have ever seen. At Montreaux we saw the Castle of Chillon. It was in this castle that the famous poem 'The prisoner of Chillon' was written by Byron. The castle was very interesting. We arrived in Interlaken a few minutes ago and tomorrow go to Lucerne and from there to Germany. Must close as the mail is going out. Wish you were here.

Lots of Love
Eunice "

LETTER FROM EUNICE TO HER PARENTS, JULY 13, 1936

Kathleen, Rose, and Joe Jr. aboard the SS *Washington*, July 1937.

Joe Jr. at the Gap of Dunloe on a trip through Killarney, Ireland, summer 1937.

Joe Jr. at the Giant's Causeway in County Antrim, Northern Ireland, summer 1937.

Kathleen and Joe Jr. at Blarney Castle in Cork, Ireland, summer 1937.

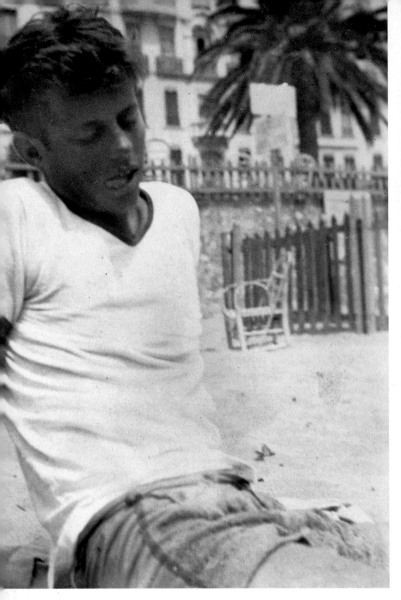

THE CAPTIONS FOR THESE PHOTOGRAPHS
WERE EXTRACTED FROM A SCRAPBOOK LEM BILLINGS
CREATED MEMORIALIZING HIS AND JACK'S
1937 EUROPEAN TOUR.

(CLOCKWISE, FROM ABOVE)

"Kennedy on the beach the morning after Cannes."
July 31, 1937.

"Reading from left to right: the Leaning Tower of Pisa &
Kennedy." August 4, 1937.

"Kennedy & the only pigeon he could attract."
August 15, 1937.

"…we also got our pictures finally taken with the pigeons
altho we had a hard time making them have any part of
Kennedy or the food he offered them." August 15, 1937.

Bronxville, New York
May 1937

"Dear Jack:

I have not heard from you about your appointment with the dentist. I am going to hold back $25.00 on your June allowance and until an appointment is made.

I hope I shall hear from you soon about Cape Cod, or I shall hold back $50.00.

Lovingly,
Mother"

LETTER TO JACK FROM HIS MOTHER

Jack and Dunker, the dachshund he bought while touring Germany with Lem Billings during August 20 to 24, 1937. Four days after purchasing Dunker for eight dollars, Jack was forced to find another home for the dog because of his allergies.

“Dear Santa Claus,

Thank you very much for the toys you gave me. You can give me some more any time you want to. I liked the watch best. Thank you again.

Lot of
Love
teddy

P. S. Happy new year. ”

LETTER FROM TEDDY TO SANTA CLAUS, CIRCA 1939

Teddy in a police costume in Palm Beach, December 1937.

Joe Jr., Kathleen, and Jack on the way to join their parents at Parliament to hear British Prime Minister Neville Chamberlain's declaration of war against Germany, September 3, 1939.

CHAPTER

4

THE EMBASSY YEARS

Jack with his grandfather Honey Fitz in Palm Beach,
circa 1938.

" Today I resigned as chairman of the Maritime Commission and was sworn in as ambassador to Great Britain. The ceremony took place in President Roosevelt's private office. Mr. Justice Reed administered the oath of office. Eddie Moore, Miss LeHand, Marvin McIntyre, Mrs. James Roosevelt and Mrs. Stanley Reed were there. "

FEBRUARY 18, 1938

" The sailing today on the *Manhattan* was a nightmare. All of the children, except Jack, were there to see me off, but I couldn't get to them. Newspaper men, casual well wishers, old friends and strangers by the thousand, it seemed to me, pressed into my cabin until we all nearly suffocated. Joe Guffey was seeing someone off and I shook hands with him. Jimmy Roosevelt managed to get to my cabin and I took him into the bedroom for a brief chat. Even there, the photographers had to snap us as we sat on the bed trying to make sense.

Finally, I got up to the deck and the children. The professional photographers were reinforced by all of the passengers who had cameras. I sent them ashore just before the gangplank was raised, Eddie Moore promising to get them a place on the dock where they could wave to me as the ship got under way. I waited on the promenade deck and saw them clearly, standing on the uncovered portion, in the rain, waving and throwing kisses. "

FEBRUARY 23, 1938

" Today, I became a full fledged ambassador by presenting my letters of credence to King George VI. The coaches, with their scarlet-coated drivers and footmen, came for us at the Embassy a little after eleven. Herschel Johnson, Millard, Williamson, Butterworth, Capt. Willson, Col. Lee, Meekins and Dr. Taylor accompanied me as my staff.

Sir Sidney Clive was in charge, and rode with me in my coach. I discussed again with him the matter of court presentations, and found that he had the jitters more than ever. It appears they feel any refusal on my part might mean the United States is snubbing the new King.

The show at Buckingham Palace was up to expectations, and I chatted informally with the King for five minutes. I found him charming in every way. Lord Halifax was there. The King said he liked to play golf, but could not for the moment because of an infected hand. He mentioned that he plays tennis left-handed. "

MARCH 8, 1938

Joe Jr., Joe, and Jack in Southampton, England,
July 2, 1938.

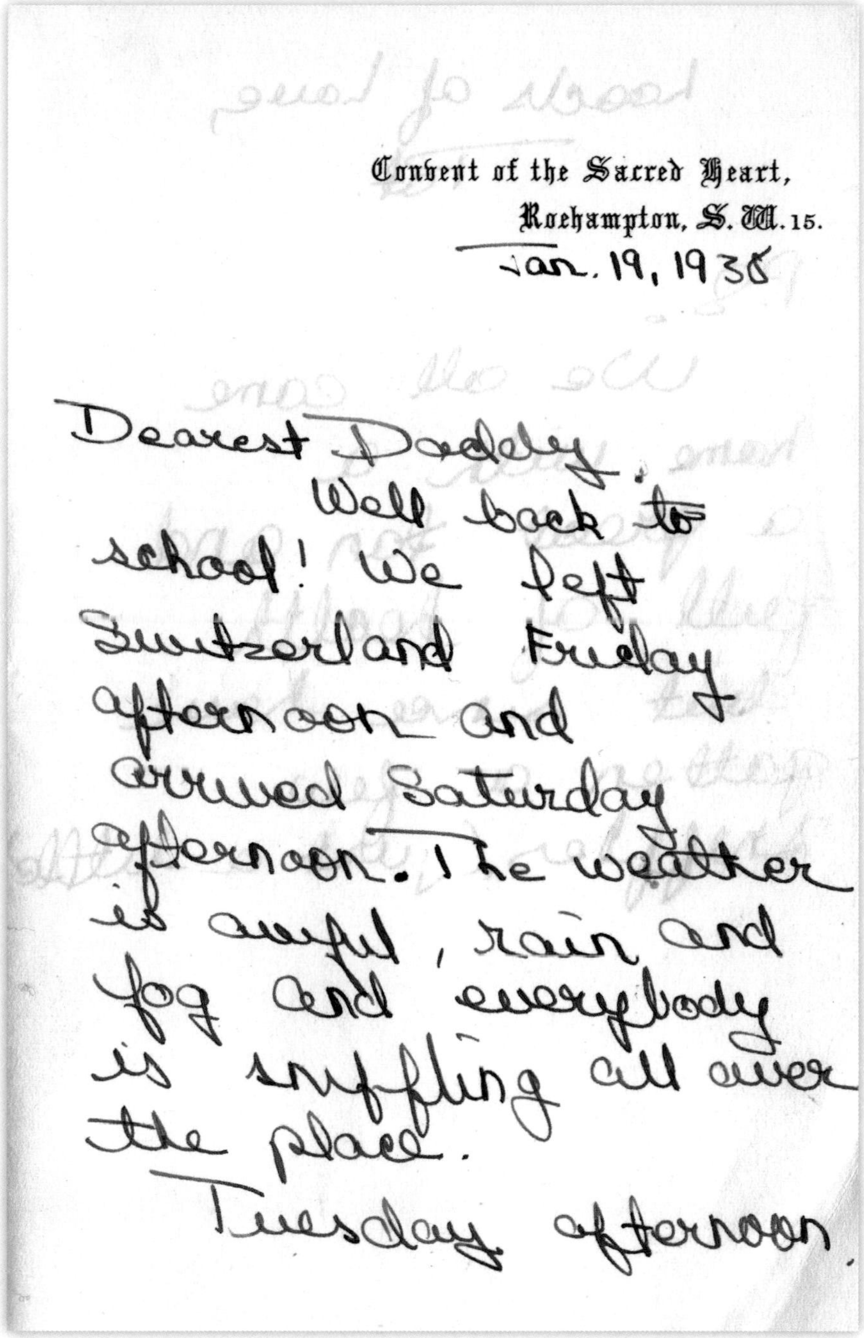

Convent of the Sacred Heart,
Roehampton, S.W. 15.

Jan. 19, 1938

Dearest Dudley,
Well back to school! We left Switzerland Friday afternoon and arrived Saturday afternoon. The weather is awful, rain and fog and everybody is sniffling all over the place.
Tuesday afternoon.

(ABOVE) Letter from Pat to her father.

NOTE: The original letter was mistakenly dated January 19, 1938. The actual date of this letter is January 19, 1939.

(OPPOSITE) Pat on board the SS *Washington*, March 1938.

(CONTINUED)

we all went to the Pantamine "Babes in the Wood". It's exactly like our theater only the story is a fairy tale. During the first and second act we all had a picture taken with the Star of the play. We all sat in the royal box.

That's about all the news. Come home soon.

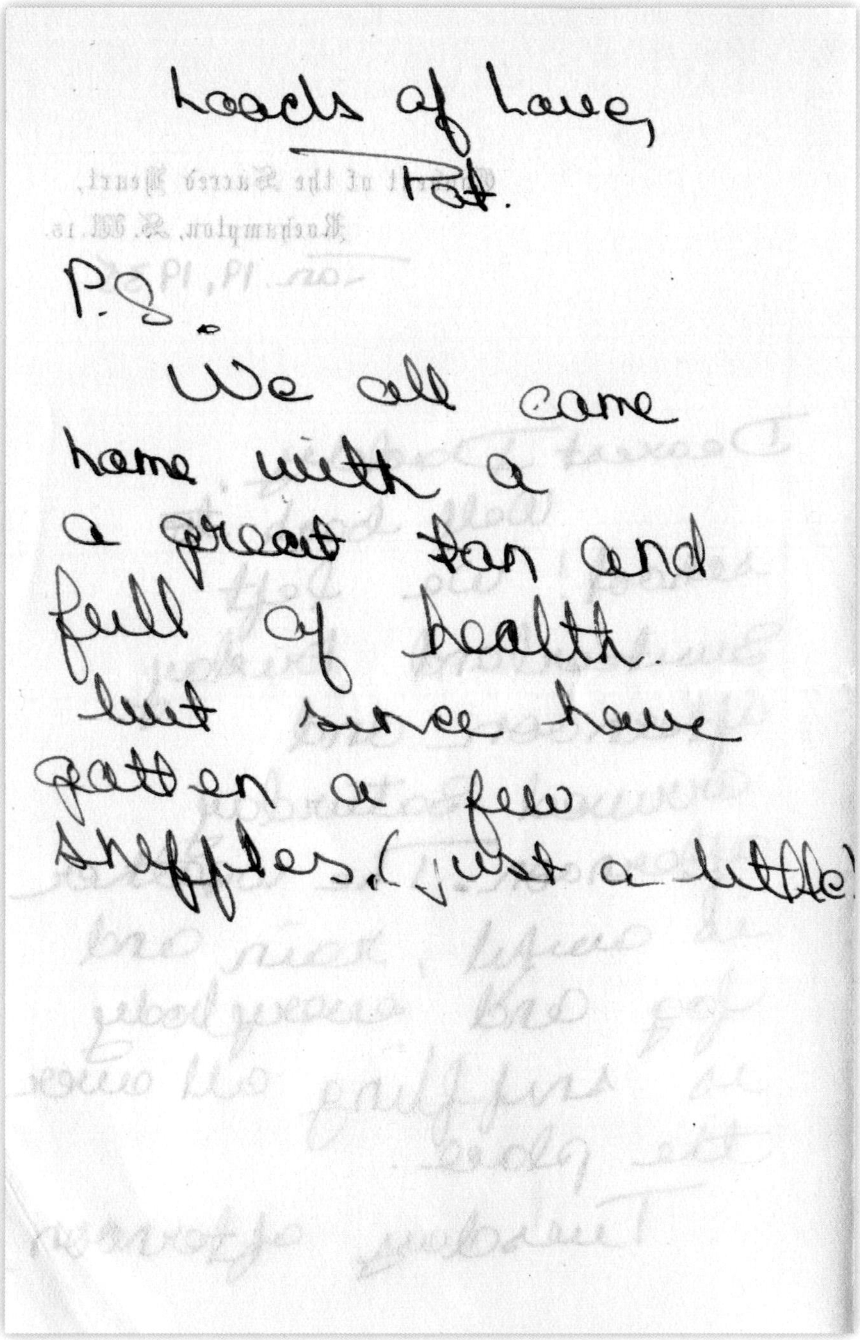

Loads of love,

Pat.

P.S.

We all came
home with a
a great tan and
full of health.
but since have
gotten a few
sniffles. (just a little!)

(ABOVE) Joe and Rose on the grounds of the ambassado-
rial residence in London, circa 1938.

(OPPOSITE) Joe Jr., Joe, and Teddy at the ambassadorial
residence in London, circa 1938.

(ABOVE) Eunice and Rose in London, prior to Eunice's
presentation at Court, July 12, 1939.

(OPPOSITE) Kathleen, Rosemary, and Rose in formal
gowns, before their presentation at the Court of St. James,
London, May 11, 1938.

Rosemary in Kilcroney, Ireland, circa 1938–1939.

(ABOVE) Joe Jr. helps Teddy with his reading at the United
States ambassador's residence in London, circa 1938–1939.

(OPPOSITE) Teddy visiting Kensington Gardens in
London, circa 1938–1939.

A PORTRAIT OF MYSELF

"I am thirteen years old, and about five feet two inches tall. I have got a lot of freckles. I have hazel eyes, and blond hair which is plenty hard to keep down because I have so many licks, and so much of it. I am not very fat, but fat enough. I weigh about one hundred pounds. I take about five and a half shoe.

I have a pretty good character on the whole, but my temper is not too good. I am not jealous of any one, I have got a very loud voice, and talk alot, but sometimes my talk is not very interesting. I have quite good tastes for food, but there is alot of things I don't like at all for instence cabbage, fish pie, Brussels sprouts, colif flower, and pears. I love almost every thing, Cholcet. I like the cinema very much, and go very often. I go to the Theatre once in a while, and like it quite well. I like football, but I like American football much better. I don't like cricket very much I like baseball alot. Going swimming is one of my favorite sports. I like skiing one of the best, and I think I am the best at this sport out of all the thing I do. I can't dive very well, but like it to a cirten exstant. I think this is a portrait of my self."

AN ESSAY BY THIRTEEN-YEAR-OLD ROBERT F. KENNEDY

(OPPOSITE) Bobby, Teddy, Sir James Calder, and Jean at the Regent's Park Zoo in London, circa 1938–1939. Sir James Calder was Ambassador Kennedy's business associate.

(THIS PAGE) Jean, Teddy, Bobby, and an unidentified friend on an elephant ride at the Regent's Park Zoo in London, circa 1938–1939.

Dec 11, 1938 Sun

Dear Daddy,

I hope, as I write this letter that the waves arn't as big as in the Popeye short we saw the other night if they are I bet Mr Houghton and Jack Kennedy are feeling plenty ill. We got a post card from an Orphonage in Italy thanking Daddy and me for the card we sent them a little while ago, Teddy was reading all morning and is thinking and talking about you. I went to a party yesterday it was

quite alot of fun. Give my love to everyone in America

Love From everybody

Bobby

P.S. Tell Jack Miss Hennessey said she loved him as much as ever

(ABOVE) Eunice, Bobby, Rosemary, Jean, Rose, and Teddy go on a sleigh ride in St. Moritz, Switzerland, Christmas 1938.

(OPPOSITE) Letter from Bobby to his father, December 11, 1938. The Jack Kennedy mentioned in line 6 refers to a business associate of Joe's, not Bobby's brother.

SUVRETTA HOUSE
St MORITZ

and it really would have been perfect if you and Jack had been here.

Joe has found no girl for himself yet although he has gone to almost every hotel in St Moritz. But

Excerpt from Eunice's letter to her father,
St. Moritz, December 26, 1938.

NOTE: Eunice is writing to her father in Palm Beach, where he and Jack celebrated the Christmas holiday while the rest of the family vacationed in St. Moritz, Switzerland. Jack was in poor health (referenced here) and was later admitted to the Mayo Clinic in Rochester, Minnesota.

The MacDonnels arrive tomorrow so we still have some hope for him.

My love to Johnny and tell him we all pray daily for his stomach

Loads of love

Eunice

PS. This pen is terrible but I cant find another

(RIGHT) The original caption written by Rose on this photograph was: "Bobby after winning the race for boys of 16 & under on New Years Day." St. Moritz, 1939.

(OPPOSITE) This photograph of Joe Jr. was made into a postcard. Postmarked 20 Jan 1939, Joe Jr. wrote to Jack, who was in the United States at the time: "Dear Brother, Switz was marvelous. Lest you forget what your Brother looks like here I Am ready to do The Cresta Run. 75 miles per hour 6 inches off The ground."

" Dear Mother,

We are enjoying it here very much. All the children are in different skiing classes, and Bob won the race on New Year's Day for children at the Suvretta House under sixteen years old so he did very well. He is remarkably good and is only one class below Joe, who was too daring and ran into a rock and had to have four or five stitches in his arm, but he is at it again.

I am taking skating lessons and can now do a figure eight. I also have a chance to speak German again as in this part of the Alps there is a great deal of German spoken.

We expect to leave here on the 13th so when I write again, it will be from the Embassy.

I imagine by now that [illegible] has seen plenty of pictures of us all again.

Hope you are planning to go South. Hope Joe will rent house, and if he does will you think whether you would like to go to Jack Daly's (Brazilian Court) or the Breakers.

Much, much love to all. I've bought the Gargans some Swiss dresses.

Devotedly
Rose

I want to thank father for check; I am not sure whether I did or not. "

LETTER FROM ROSE TO HER MOTHER, CIRCA JANUARY 1939

EXCERPTS FROM TEDDY'S DIARY

" This morning I went out skiing with all the rest of the Kennedys. Jean waited for me & she and I went over to the new Nursery slopes to practice. I fell down on the way over & I started crying because I couldn't get my skiis straightened, so Jean came & helped me. It had snowed the night before, so the snow on top was so soft, That when you fell you got all covered with snow, but you did not hurt yourself very much. "

JANUARY 7, 1939

" Today it was snowing a little in the morning, & it snowed very hard in the afternoon, but just the same all us Kennedys went out ski-ing. Jean & I always go together because Bob & Pat & Eunice go up on the ski-lift. They are very good skiers, & we are not. I had a very good time & fell down lots but I always got up myself. "

JANUARY 10, 1939

Jean, Rose, and Teddy on the slopes of St. Moritz,
Christmas 1938.

Kathleen, Pat, Bobby, Jack, Rose, Joe, Teddy, Eunice, Jean, and Rosemary at the Vatican, March 13, 1939.

"This morning we all dressed in black, but I had my blue suit on, and we went to the Vatican to have a private audience with the Pope. We had our photographs taken outside the hotel before we left. Then we drove to the Vatican, & when we passed thru the gates that lead to where the Pope lives, all the guards saluted us. Mr. Galeazzi met us & took us up in the lift & then he brought us into a room where we took off our coats & gloves. There were about 10 men in this room that were all dressed in red, red shoes, breeches & coats & they all tried to help us. Then we went thru a hall and there were a lot of Swiss guards in a line & they were dressed in orange, red & blue striped uniforms. They were very big, straight men & they stood 'at attention' when we went by. Then we went thru 3 or 4 rooms & then we came to a big room where the Pope's throne was, so we all took out all our rosaries, pictures & medals & put them on a tray. Some of us kept a few rosaries over our arm. The throne was gold & red. We waited here for a while, because Daddy was in another room talking with the Pope. Soon we were told to go in & we marched in a line & all knelt on one knee before the Pope. Then each one went up & knelt down & kissed Pope Pius' ring. He was dressed all in white. When everybody had kissed his ring, he talked to us a few minutes. He gave us each a rosary & he gave mother one in a large white box. Mother said that we were going to have a marble slab put near the place where he sat when he visited us in Bronxville when he was Cardinal Pacelli. He smiled, & he said he would like to see us all again & asked if we were happy in London. He blessed us about 7 times. Soon it was time to go, so we all walked out of the door backwards, because Mr. Galeazzi said you should never turn your back to the Pope. After we went out, Mr. Gowan brought all our holiest things into be blessed. Then we went downstairs & in one long corridor we had our pictures taken, & then Mr. Galeazzi brought us to see the Sixtine [sic] Chapel. There was a large painting at one end by Michaelangelo [sic] & the ceiling had a lot of paintings on it. Then we went into a room & met the Sec. of State who was a Cardinal. Then we went out into the yard & we took some movies & then came home & had lunch…"

EXCERPT FROM TEDDY'S DIARY, MARCH 13, 1939

" Woke up at 8 to get ready for audience with Pope at 11:30.

Got the family all together in three cars with Miss Dunn and Miss Hennessey, the Moores, Houghton, Gowen and Mrs. Kennedy, French maid. Guided by Galeazzi, started for Vatican. On arrival we were photographed…

The Pope was in his old office. He had not moved to the Pope's quarters as yet. We went into the room and genuflected and then to my amazement as he was sitting behind a table he got up and I went to meet him he advanced a few steps towards me. I knelt and kissed his ring and then stood up. He smiled, motioned me to sit down and then sat down himself…

Then the family came in and all knelt and kissed the ring and he talked with Rose and remembered Teddy…Then he walked over to the table, a thing a Pope never does and got a white box with rosary which he gave to Rose with his blessing. He talked to her so much and so kindly and intimately I thought she would faint. He then gave rosaries in white casings to all the children. After 15 minutes we all knelt for his blessing and as we withdrew he said 'Pray for me.' "

EXCERPT FROM JOSEPH P. KENNEDY SR.'S DIARY, MARCH 13, 1939

"This morning I got up at half past six, because I was making my First Holy Communion at the Pope's chapel at the Vatican @ 7:30 Mass. Eunice, Pat, Jack Daddy & Mr. Galeazzi went with me. I wore a white tie, a white bow on my left arm, my blue suit & long black stockings & black shoes. When we got to the place, we went up on the lift & then we went into a room that I had never been in before & we left our coats there. Then right off this room was a little Chapel. This is where the Pope says Mass every day. It was terribly small, and only 5 of us were allowed in there, because it was so small. We got there a little while before Mass, so we all prayed. Soon the Pope came in and he put on all his vestments right in the Chapel, in front of the altar. Then he said Mass. He was all dressed in red and white. At Communion, the Pope came down to your seat and gave us all Holy Communion. Then he went back to the altar & finished Mass. After Mass, one of the 3 Nuns who were there brought out a present for me on a plate & put it on a chair & then she touched the Holy Father's arm & I guess he knew that she had gotten the present alright. So then he went over & got it & gave it to me. He made the sign of the Cross on my forehead and said 'Keep this for a souvenir, and be good & pious during your life.' It was a lovely silver rosary and he blessed it right in front of us. He spoke for a while to Eunice & Pat about how good they were to come from Naples to be at His Mass, but I didn't pay much attention because he wasn't talking to me. Then the Pope went out, & we started out too, but soon the one that served Mass, came up to us and gave me the candle and lily that had been burning in front of my seat all during Mass. Daddy said he was going to have the lily waxed so that it would last. Then we went back to the Excelsior Hotel and Jack took some pictures of me…"

EXCERPT FROM TEDDY'S DIARY, MARCH 16, 1939

Teddy on the occasion of his First Communion, Rome,
March 16, 1939.

Pat, Teddy, and Eunice in Rome,
March 16, 1939.

"After we arrived the Pope walked in looking neither to the right or left and proceeded to put on his vestments standing in front of the altar. The vestments were red and he wore red shoes.

His valet acted as altar boy.

I noticed when the wine and water were served to him he poured a good deal of wine and then used a gold spoon to put the water in the chalice.

When it came time for Communion he left the altar, came down to Teddy and gave him his Communion. His touch was so light when he put the Host on his tongue he didn't quite know it was there. I knew this was so because when he put it on my tongue I had a like experience."

EXCERPT FROM JOSEPH P. KENNEDY SR.'S DIARY, MARCH 16, 1939

Teddy observes the troops of Italian dictator Benito
Mussolini, Rome, March 14, 1939.

"This morning, the guide took us to see Mussolini forum. There were many
soldiers exercising here. There is a large place like the coloseum that is being built,
+ there is a swimming pool, tennis court, a fencing gallery + a place to run races
that has a lot of statues + these statues were given by different towns in Italy."

EXCERPT FROM TEDDY'S DIARY, MARCH 14, 1939

Jack riding a camel in Egypt, Spring 1939. Jack was granted a leave of absence from Harvard during the second semester of the 1939 academic year to have a firsthand look at the growing European situation. The observations he gathered during this period helped shape his senior thesis, which was later published as *Why England Slept*.

The Kennedy family at Eden Roc. Back row: Kathleen, Joe Jr., Rosemary, Rose, and Teddy. Middle row: Jack, Eunice, Joe, and Pat. Front row: Bobby and Jean. Cannes, August 1939.

Joe Jr., Jack, and Bobby greet their father upon his return
from England, December 1939.

Dear Teddy:

…I don't know whether you would have very much excitement during these raids. I am sure, of course, you wouldn't be scared, but if you heard all these guns firing every night and the bombs bursting you might get a little fidgety. I am sure you would have liked to be with me and seen the fires the German bombers started in London. It is really terrible to think about, and all those poor women and children and homeless people down in the East End of London all seeing their places destroyed. I hope when you grow up you will dedicate your life to trying to work out plans to make people happy instead of making them miserable, as war does today…

Well, old boy, write me some letters and I want you to know that I miss seeing you a lot, for after all, you are my pal, aren't you?

Love,
Dad

EXCERPT OF A LETTER FROM JOSEPH P. KENNEDY SR. TO TEDDY

Teddy and his father, Joseph P. Kennedy Sr., at the
United States ambassadorial residence in London,
England, circa 1939.

(ABOVE) Pat in Palm Beach, Christmas 1939.

(OPPOSITE) Kathleen and Jack in Palm Beach,
Christmas 1939.

Jack on the day of his graduation from
Harvard University, June 1940.

" His attitudes about dress and appearance were apt to be equally offhand. We have a snapshot of him at the time he graduated from Harvard, in his black academic gown, with a suitably serious expression, but with his feet in a pair of worn brown-and-white saddle shoes… "

ROSE DESCRIBES JACK ON THE DAY OF HIS HARVARD GRADUATION

Hyannis Port, June 24, 1940

" Dear Joe,

We went up to the Class Day on Wednesday; Rose, Eunice, Bob, and I, and were joined by Kathleen up there. We went directly to lunch in the Yard. Jack was as usual entirely irresponsible when he talked to me Tuesday night. He thought we could go to Dutchland for lunch. We arrived about 15 minutes ahead, and Torb [Torbert MacDonald] came out and took us to a couple of gates where we were checked up for tickets which we did not have and he referred them to Jack. We had a hurried lunch, and Jack was greeted by several of the waitresses who served him solicitously, and seemed anxious that he should have something good to eat; however, he decided he should leap out and get something suitable for his tummy, and then decided everything was in a rush any way and that he should be on his way to join his class. We then swallowed our lunch and made for the stadium and had no tickets again and bought some and clammered up the stairs. The festivities there were as usual. There was a speech made suggesting the probability of the present graduating class going into war and there was considerable hissing. Otherwise, everything went on as usual. I did not see anyone I knew…

At 9 the next morning Jack phoned and urged us to come out at once. We stopped at Spee Club for our tickets. Jack popped out and we got at the Quadrangle where our seats were. They were the worst in the place; three rows from the back on the extreme left; however, we had the brave idea of moving back against the college wall where it was sunny. As it happened, all the dignitaries & the graduates passed along that particular section on their way to the platform so we had a marvelous view of everyone. Kick was sure he had chosen the seats for this, but I am sure he got them at the last minute.

He was really very handsome in his cap and gown as he had a tan which made him look healthy and he has got a wonderful smile. After graduation, we returned to his room where after waiting several minutes and not finding him, we left and went in town…

All my love dearest,
Rosa "

LETTER FROM ROSE TO HER HUSBAND

Ambassador Kennedy poses outside of 14 Prince's Gate in London, England, holding a copy of Jack's book, *Why England Slept*, which was published during the summer of 1940.

Jack in Hyannis Port, circa 1940–1941.

Teddy and Joe Jr. in Palm Beach, circa 1939–1940.

Joe Jr. on Cape Cod in the summer of 1940, in a rare color
photo from this period.

(ABOVE) Joe Jr. with his grand-uncle Henry Fitzgerald (left) and his grandfather John "Honey Fitz" Fitzgerald during the 1940 presidential campaign.

(OPPOSITE) Joe Jr., one of four delegates representing Massachusetts's Ninth Congressional District, at the 1940 Democratic National Convention held in Chicago, Illinois, July 15–18, 1940.

Palm Beach

March 1940

" Joe dear,

I have a definite idea that it would be a wonderful feat if you could put over the idea that although you are against America's entering the war—still you are encouraging help to England in some way. It seems to me most people in America would be sympathetic to that idea and it would endear you to the hearts of the British. It may be impractical, but I have felt it strongly the last two weeks.

Much love, darling, and I hope you're O.K.,

Rosa "

LETTER FROM ROSE TO HER HUSBAND

Rose and Joe in Palm Beach, February 16, 1940.

Rose and Joe in Bronxville, November 1940.

"Dear Rose:

I have a chance to get this letter off on the CLARE going Wednesday, so I thought I would bring you up to date. It is really a great consolation to talk to you on Sunday nights, because as you may imagine, desperate as it is for you folks, it is much worse for me here…Also I know you will be terribly sorry to hear that Roehampton Convent has been bombed twice, and quite badly damaged. I talked with Mother Isabel also, and she told me an incendiary bomb dropped in the yard at Boxmoor, but no damage was done. It is almost impossible to meet anybody, no matter where they live, who has not had a bad experience with this bombing or who is not intimately acquainted with somebody who has suffered some loss. Jack Kennedy's boss, Hanbury, was killed with his entire family by a bomb last Friday night. So you see there are things happening which bring this terrible mess home to one every day.

I can't help but think of those days before Munich and all during the next year, when I deplored what this war was going to do to all of us. You will remember how often I said my real reason for not wanting England to get into a war was because of the terrible effect it would eventually have on the United States. Well, it is having that effect, and it is going to continue to have it…

As to the situation here, of course we have had acute bombings and several very disagreeable day light raids, particularly in Bristol, Liverpool and Southampton. A great deal more damage is being done here than is given out to the Press, but the greatest danger I see is from forcing all the inhabitants of London into air-raid shelters at night where they sleep with their clothes on, sitting up, lying down—any way, and all crowded together. If we don't have the worst epidemics of disease before this winter is thru, I'll miss my guess. The ground is laid for some terrible results.

As far as I am concerned, I seem to be going on reasonably well. I wouldn't know what it was not to go to bed and not hear motors droning over my head or gun fire all over the place. I ride horseback and play golf with German planes flying overhead on their way to some place, and in spite of it all I am still very well. The strain, I think, is on the mental processes rather than on the physical ones…

Well, dear, I think that is about all the news at the minute. As I said, I am planning, unless something dreadful happens, to be with you this month. I haven't much to say for all the children, but I am sure you will tell them all the news I have written you.

All my love, darling.

Joe"

EXCERPT OF A LETTER FROM JOSEPH P. KENNEDY SR. TO ROSE

Lt.(jg) John F. Kennedy and Ensign Joseph P. Kennedy Jr.,
December 1942.

THE WAR
YEARS

The 1940s were a tumultuous decade for the Kennedys, along with millions of American families whose lives would be utterly changed by World War II. American involvement in the war lasted from 1941 to 1945; sixteen million Americans participated in the war effort, and more than four hundred thousand Americans were killed. The aftermath effects of the war would last far beyond the decade.

As the war effort ramped up, the Kennedy family was in transition. Joe returned from London to the United States in the fall of 1940, and was called upon to testify before Congress that winter about the war. With the older children all out of the house and the younger ones at boarding school, Joe and Rose sold the Bronxville house in 1941, and then divided their time between Hyannis Port and Palm Beach. Aware that the impending war would disrupt their lives, Rose took Eunice on a cruise to the Caribbean and then on to Rio de Janeiro in Brazil that spring, where they were joined briefly by Jack. Having spent a semester at Stanford University auditing business courses in the fall of 1940, Jack had decided that the business world was not for him, and he was "having a hard time deciding on a career," Rose wrote.

The summer of 1941 was the last summer the entire Kennedy family would be together. Rose remembered the ambiance of the house in Hyannis Port that summer, with a cacophony of radios and phonographs operating morning, noon, and night, along with ringing telephones, barking dogs, the bounce of tennis balls, splashing in the ocean, and the cries of welcome and farewell.

The year 1941 also saw the tragic decline of Rosemary, who, despite being born with an intellectual disability, had led a fairly active life. As her condition deteriorated, specialists recommended a new procedure that they considered promising. When the lobotomy performed on Rosemary went tragically wrong, Joe and Rose made the heart-wrenching decision to send her to St. Coletta's School in Jefferson, Wisconsin, where she could receive proper care for the remainder of her life.

With war looming, Joe Jr. decided not to return for his final year at Harvard Law School and instead signed up for the naval aviation cadet program, earning his wings in May 1942. Then Jack enlisted in the navy. After attending the Naval Reserve Midshipman's School at Northwestern University during the summer of 1942, Jack requested assignment to a motor torpedo boat squadron in the South Pacific.

When the Japanese bombed Pearl Harbor on December 7, 1941, Joseph P. Kennedy Sr. immediately sent a telegram to President Roosevelt, writing, "Mr. President, in this great crisis all Americans are with you. Name the battle post. I'm yours to command." But the president never responded, and Joe

Back row: Rose, Teddy, and Jean. Front row: Pat, Bobby, and Kathleen. Joe appears in the doorway. Hyannis Port, summer 1941.

Kennedy waited on the sidelines, "suffering in silence," as he wrote to a colleague in Britain.

Jack left the United States for the South Pacific on March 6, 1943, as a lieutenant in command of a motor torpedo boat, the PT 109. Jack and his crew of twelve men were assigned to patrol the waters of the Solomon Islands and stop Japanese ships from delivering supplies to their soldiers stationed there. On the night of August 2, 1943, PT 109 was suddenly rammed at full speed by the Japanese destroyer *Amagiri*. The impact split the PT 109 in half and two of Jack's men were killed instantly. The others managed to jump overboard as their boat went up in flames. Their subsequent ordeal and Jack's heroic efforts to save his surviving crew members, despite his

own injuries, became famous at the time as the subject of several news stories. After their rescue and a brief period of recuperation, Jack requested and was granted the command of another patrol boat, the PT 59.

In June 1944, Jack was awarded the Navy and Marine Corps Medal for his leadership and courage, and was honorably discharged from the navy in March 1945.

Joe Jr. was in England, having been stationed there in September 1943. By June 1944, he had flown thirty missions, which completed his tour of duty and made him eligible to return to the United States. However, in late July, Joe Jr. wrote to his parents that he was postponing his return home and had volunteered for a top secret mission, later identified as Operation Aphrodite, "that is safe and there is no need to worry." Operation Aphrodite was intended to cripple the Nazi V-2 rocket-building program. Joe Jr. also wrote in a similar vein to Jack on August 10, 1944: "…Tell the family not to get excited about my staying over here. I am not repeat not contemplating marriage nor intending to risk my fine neck…in any crazy venture."

In the early evening of August 12, 1944, Joe Jr. with his copilot, Wilford (Bud) Willy, took off for the last time in a PB4Y Liberator, which was packed with explosives. Somewhere over the English Channel, the explosives prematurely detonated, destroying the bomber and killing both men.

After leaving Finch College in 1941, Kathleen began working for the *Washington Times-Herald*, in Washington, D.C., and was eventually promoted to reviewing plays and movies under her own byline. However, she wanted to help in the war effort and soon joined the Red Cross. On June 25, 1943, she left America and set sail for England, where she was to assume her official position as the program assistant at Hans Crescent, a club in London that offered food, supplies, and accommodations for officers. Once back in London, Kick resumed her acquaintance with old friends, especially William (Billy) Cavendish, the Marquess of Hartington, and the son of the Duke and Duchess of Devonshire. Kick and Billy's relationship developed quickly and they

decided to marry. After months of careful deliberation and much opposition from both their families because of religious differences, Kick agreed to wed Billy, an Anglican. On the morning of May 6, 1944, Kick, accompanied by her older brother, Joe Jr., made her way to a London registry office. There in a private ceremony, surrounded by Joe Jr., a few friends, and Billy's family, Kathleen Kennedy married William John Robert Cavendish, the Marquess of Hartington.

After a wedding reception at the home of Lord Hambleden in Eaton Square, Kick and Billy traveled to Compton Place in Eastbourne, where they were to spend part of their honeymoon. Like most war brides, Kick's time with her new husband was relatively short, and within five weeks Billy was called back to the battlefield. On their last evening together, Billy recorded the following entry in their diary:

June 13th
"'This time tomorrow where shall I be, not in this academy.'

Although I've been expecting it daily, it is quite a shock now that it has come. I shall always remember this last month as the most perfect of my life.

How beastly it is always to be ending things. This war seems to cause nothing but goodbyes. I think that that is the worst part of it, worse even than fighting."

Kick completed Billy's diary entry with her own thoughts: "This is the saddest evening. Ever since May 6th I have had a wonderful sense of contentment. B is most perfect husband."

In September, Kick, who had returned to the United States to join her mourning family in Hyannis Port after learning of Joe Jr.'s death, received the devastating news that Billy had been killed in battle in Belgium on September 10, 1944. Arrangements were quickly made for Kick to return to England to be with the Devonshires during their time of grief. After Billy's death, Kathleen made London her permanent residence.

While the war years had brought tragedy to the Kennedy family, there were many accomplishments for the younger children. Having previously attended Manhattanville College in New York, Eunice transferred to Stanford University, receiving a bachelor of science degree in sociology in 1943. Following graduation, she served in the Special War Problems Division of the Department of State.

Pat attended Rosemont College in Rosemont, Pennsylvania, and became interested in the theater. She received a bachelor of arts degree from Rosemont in 1945. After graduation, Pat decided to pursue her interest in theatrical activities and began working as an assistant in NBC's New York production department.

Bobby attended Milton Academy and entered the V-12 program for naval training. He served aboard the USS *Lt. Joseph P. Kennedy, Jr.*, a newly commissioned navy destroyer that had been christened by Joe Jr.'s goddaughter, Jean, in 1945.

Like her older sisters before her, Jean was enrolled at Sacred Heart in Noroton, Connecticut. Teddy, who had attended a variety of schools since the sale of the Bronxville estate, was enrolled at the Fessenden School in Waltham, Massachusetts. Since Waltham was less than twenty miles from Boston, Teddy was able to enjoy regular visits with his maternal grandfather, Honey Fitz.

"As the youngest in my family, and with my family on the move in the 1940s, a lot of my schooling was done in boarding schools. My junior high years were spent at the Fessenden School in Newton, Massachusetts. Newton is a suburb of Boston, and Grandpa lived nearby in the Bellevue Hotel in downtown Boston. Boarding school can be a lonely place at any age, as you are separated from your family, so you can imagine how happy I was to have Grandpa as someone to visit and do things with when I had time off from school. In so many ways, Grandpa was a second parent for me. He was someone who would listen to my adolescent chatter, my hopes and dreams, and he would be my personal guide as we explored the city of Boston. We would often eat lunch or dinner in the hotel dining room, but I never got much to eat. Grandpa was always introducing me to someone sitting nearby or taking me into the kitchen so the staff could meet me as well. Grandpa simply knew everyone, and if he didn't, he acted as if he knew them anyway.

Grandpa loved the city and took great pride in the things he had done for the citizens of Boston when he was mayor—things like the zoo, the Christmas tree on the Common, the Park Street bandstand, things that everyone could enjoy. He was very conscious of the welfare of everyone. He also took great pride in the history of the city, which he saw on every street corner and down every alley. He wanted me to appreciate his sense of history as well, so a one-time visit to the USS *Constitution* or to Bunker Hill or to Paul Revere's house was never enough. We would go back over and over again, and he would tell the same story over and over again. In time, I would become his guide, and he was quite pleased with the progress I was making in capturing the moment, the event or the place we were looking at. Being a good oral historian takes time and practice. And being a good Irish storyteller is a gift you hone. I think I did quite well, at least according to Grandpa…

With so many grandchildren, I suppose one might wonder, did he have a favorite? He did—the one he was with at that moment. He had that special gift of making you feel you were the only person in the whole world he cared about. As a kid, to have an adult pay that kind of attention to you was very special. How nice that was for all of us to be able to feel that way when we were with him. As I've said, for me he was a second parent at a time in my life when I needed one the most."

TEDDY, ON SPENDING TIME WITH HIS GRANDFATHER FITZGERALD

Eunice, Pat, Rose, Jean, Teddy, Joe, and Bobby,
in Palm Beach, circa 1941.

" Henry Ward Beecher wrote, 'A mother's heart is a child's schoolroom.' My mother was my greatest teacher. She made me laugh. She helped me to learn, and in learning, I experienced love. She kept maps around the house and always quizzed me: 'Now Eunice, where is Pakistan? Where is Wales?...'

She knew many poems by heart and cherished Longfellow's poem about Paul Revere. All her children followed her example and memorized it—except one. She taught us to listen to Dad's dinner table conversations about politics—conversations which seemed boring to a small child but later became the basis for so much of what we did in life. She sparked my imagination with bedtime stories, excerpts from *Little Women*, *Black Beauty*, and, of course, the Gospels...

One thing she wanted all her life, and sought it every day, was learning. I remember being at Stanford University and she came to visit me for a month. She asked me what course I was taking. I told her I was taking a course on South America. Instead of playing golf or bridge, she told me: 'I think I'll ask your professor if I can attend the course.' He said, 'Fine.' She quietly sat in the back of the room every morning listening, and then at dinner—I should have expected it—began asking me questions about the lectures. Two years later, she and I went off to Brazil; she said she had learned about Brazil and now she wanted to see it for herself. "

RECOLLECTIONS BY EUNICE ABOUT HER MOTHER

" Climbed the Christ (statue that dominates Rio) by car. Fascinates me because one can see top at night approaching city as well as day. Always seem to be climbing in South America on funicular or by car. "

RECOLLECTIONS BY ROSE ABOUT HER TRIP TO BRAZIL

(OPPOSITE) Rose and Eunice sitting on the stairs leading to the statue of Christ the Redeemer at Mount Corcovado in Rio de Janeiro, May 1941.

(ABOVE) Rose, Jack, and Eunice in Rio de Janeiro, Brazil, May 1941.

Eunice and Joe at the Kennedy home in Hyannis Port, summer 1941.

Eunice and Rose in Hyannis Port, summer 1941.

“ Wonderfully well coordinated and with quick reflexes, one of the best athletes in our active family. A ‘talker’ with a special way of expressing herself in a pithy and witty manner that made her one of the livelier participants in our family conversations. But she was also a good listener, and marvelously generous in her interest in others, especially her brothers and sisters, but including waifs, strays, and anybody who needed her. And so through vigor, candor, wit, and comprehending sympathy she endeared herself to all of us. A special girl, no one like her. ”

ROSE’S DESCRIPTION OF EUNICE

(ABOVE) Pat in "uniform" in Hyannis Port,
circa 1941–1942

(OPPOSITE) Letter from Pat to her brother Jack,
July 10, 1942.

HYANNISPORT
MASSACHUSETTS

July 10, 1942

Dear Jack,

Well how's every little thing with you good looking. That was a wonderful speech you made on the fourth I guess you really

(CONTINUED)

are a bore. Too bad
your sister isn't.
The Cape is
duller than ever and
your sister more
unpopular (if that's
possible). There is
no senior racing at
the port and Bobby
is racing at Hyannis
Whitney Wright's is
the only other senior
in the port. Your
sister is now

Commodore, Secretary and Treasurer of the Yacht Club and she is going out of her mind literally. Only three boats showed up for the 4th of July race (2 of their own) So the port is really going to pot.

(CONTINUED)

Nancy Tenney is here for a month and Kick arrives tomorrow after her little trip to see Johnny before he goes in the Navy. Eunice's 21st birthday is Friday (Don't forget) and a big celebration is to be had. Too bad you can't be here.

Do you think you
will be down again.
Well kid that's
about all the news
Write soon

Lots of love
Pat.

(LEFT TO RIGHT)

Joe Jr. observes his younger siblings at play in the pool: Teddy, Jean, and Kathleen in Palm Beach, Christmas 1941.

Teddy and Kathleen in the pool in Palm Beach, Christmas 1941.

Joe Jr., Rose, and Jack in Palm Beach, circa 1942.

Jack and Rose (center) with her parents, Mary Josephine (left, standing) and Honey Fitz, and sisters-in-law Loretta Connolly and Margaret Burke in Palm Beach, circa 1942.

Jack, Honey Fitz, and Joe Jr. in Palm Beach, circa 1942.

Joe, Teddy, and Rose on the day of Teddy's Confirmation,
Palm Beach, May 1942.

March 27, 1942

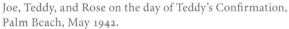 Dear Children:

…Bobby returned on Monday and he and Jean are about the same. I cannot seem to get them to meet anyone or talk very long or very loud. However, next year I think someone will come along with Bobby, which I now am convinced is a great help.

Jean goes up from here about the 13th, returning to Eden Hall, and Teddy, who is the direct antithesis of the other two, returns to Riverdale on the 6th. To Bobby's amazement when he saw him at dancing school, Teddy knows all the steps from the zomba to the old fashioned waltz. He also scans the movie columns, makes his dates, and goes confidently off without bothering anyone…

Much love to you all.

Mother

EXCERPT OF A LETTER FROM ROSE KENNEDY TO HER CHILDREN

"I'm sure it's normal for girls to look up to older brothers with some admiration and sense of dazzlement, but in our case it was fairly extreme. To us they were marvelous creatures, practically God-like, and we yearned to please them and be acceptable. Not that any of us would necessarily show it in any overt way, and nothing sugary, which would have turned them off and wasn't our style anyway. But we had this great feeling about them—as they did about us—as we all did about one another—and part of it was that they were such fun to be with. They treated us in a loving but offhand way, occasionally sternly bawling us out, but most of the time considerately and humorously, and affectionately."

EUNICE DESCRIBING THE RELATIONSHIP
BETWEEN THE KENNEDY SISTERS AND THEIR OLDER BROTHERS

Jack and Eunice in Palm Beach, circa 1942.

(ABOVE, AND OPPOSITE) Jack in his Navy dress whites, circa 1942.

Joe Jr. at the Naval Air Station in
Jacksonville, Florida, May 4, 1942.

(ABOVE) Joseph P. Kennedy Jr. receiving his commission
from his father in Jacksonville, Florida, May 5, 1942.

(OPPOSITE) Ensign Joseph P. Kennedy Jr., circa May 1942.

A pantsless Jack with his former Harvard
roommate, Torbert MacDonald, in
Hyannis Port, circa 1942.

Thursday

" Dear Jack,

Here is wire I forgot to send.

Mother is so anxious to have a picture of you in your uniform.

Do have one taken for her birthday. July 22nd.

Really do this as she longs to have one and it means so much.

Much love
Kick "

LETTER FROM KATHLEEN TO HER BROTHER JACK

Bobby, Rose, and Pat at the Kennedy
home in Hyannis Port, circa 1942.

May 13, 1943

"Dear Children:

...I received Mother's Day cards from Eunice and Bobby, which are now sitting on my bureau. I had told the girls not to send me any flowers as my plans were so upset and it is so difficult to do things these days. I was amazed and very much delighted yesterday on receiving a lovely basket full of the sweetest spring flowers. It seems Jack had written to Paul Murphy and asked him to send it to me for Mother's Day. He also enclosed a card, 'To Mother with Love. Sorry I am not there to give these personally.' It was in his own writing so imagine how thrilled I was...

Much love to all of you.
Mother "

EXCERPT OF A LETTER FROM ROSE KENNEDY TO HER CHILDREN

Jack and unidentified friends while stationed on the Solomon Islands in the South Pacific, 1943.

Jack in the Solomon Islands, 1943.

Jack and Paul "Red" Fay on the Solomon Islands in the South Pacific, 1943.

Jack on PT 109 in the Solomon Islands, 1943.

" Dear Folks:
This is just a short note to tell you that I am alive—and *not* kicking—in spite of any reports that you may happen to hear. It was believed otherwise for a few days—so reports or rumors may have gotten back to you. Fortunately they misjudged the durability of a Kennedy—and am back at the base now—and am OK. As soon as possible I shall try to give you the whole story.

Much love to you all
Jack "

LETTER FROM JACK TO HIS PARENTS FOLLOWING
THE PT 109 RESCUE, AUGUST 12, 1943

The PT 109 crew off Guadalcanal, July 1943. The crew
has been tentatively identified as follows. Back row: Allen
Webb, Leon Drawdy, Edgar Mauer, Edmund Drewitch,
John Maguire, and Jack. Front row: Charles Harris,
Maurice Kowal, Andrew Kirksey, and Lenny Thom.

(ABOVE) Joe Jr. and his crew. Back row: B. E. Cook,
G. Dowdey, Joe Jr. holding the dog named Dunkeswell,
G. P. Rapp, and B. Dodge. Front row: W. O. Dunning,
R. F. Corcoran, W. Jones, J. E. Butler, and F. T. Guseman.
Dunkeswell Aerodrome, England, circa 1943–1944.

(OPPOSITE) Letter from Joe Jr. to his sister Pat,
December 11, 1943.

Dec II, I943

England

Pat mine:

Up to this point, I havent had much news of you, except that
Mother was going up to see about you changing schools. I think, Smith
Wellsley, Vassaar or Sarah Lawrence would all be good, and needless to
say would be glad to get that   lovely, lovely lovely, Miss Patricia
Kennedy.

Life over here has cut my well rounded contours rather
sharply. We fare a good deal better, than the English, but still
we could use a good deal of the produce gleaned from the Kennedy
farm. I have written to ma mere several times about sending me
goodies, but to this point, I have existed by nibbling at packages
received by other members of the hut. Why dont you get right into
the kitchen, and whip me up a batch of fudge.

Romance is unknown in the life of this romantic, dashing
naval airman. I have now decided to center my offensive upon
personnel of this station, and start ~~an~~ onslaught upon some poor
unsuspecting Wafaf. I shall let you know the result of the encounter.
If the result is the same as many of past encounters, I shall not
let you know the result.

Most of the other fellows have heard about my beautiful
sisters, so I think I could bring home a few prospects for a very
nominal sum. Whatever became of the FBI man.???

As you are the most obvious candidate to be sporting my
chrysler aound PB this winter, I bgeg of you not t hit any more
curbs. I plan to drive it around a bit when the lights go on again,
and the shape in which I found it, after my trip out west, bodes ill
for any subsequent war usage. My love to you, honey

Merry Xmas Joe

January 9, 1944

" Dear Mr. Kennedy:

This is just a note to accompany the Purple Heart award for Jack. I am sending this to you as he's probably running around visiting and generally making up for his somewhat restricted existence out here. Hence, you can probably serve him with this, in fact, spring it on him in a family presentation.

Also, I want to tender a word of praise for Jack. We all regard ourselves fortunate indeed in knowing him as a friend, as he really is, in really the only words to express it—a swell guy. This regard is based entirely on his performance as we knew him. Jack never accepted any merits he did not actually earn. He performed all of his duties conscientiously and with admirable ease. He won the respect of officers and men alike by his disregard of himself and a quiet effective courage that manifested itself many times.

Jack has been recommended for a decoration for his work out here and I sincerely hope he will hear of it soon. He certainly deserves it.

I hope this doesn't sound like an official report, but I did want you and your family to know how very proud of your son you can be.

Give 'Shafty' [Jack] my regards and best wishes to you, sir. He is a fine lad though he does seem to have Democratic inclinations.

Republicanly yours,
A. P. Cluster
Lt. U.S.N. "

LETTER FROM LIEUTENANT A. P. CLUSTER
TO JOSEPH P. KENNEDY SR.

" For heroism in the rescue of three men following the ramming and sinking of his motor torpedo boat while attempting a torpedo attack on a Japanese destroyer in the Solomon Islands area on the night of August 1–2, 1943. Lieutenant KENNEDY, Captain of the boat, directed the rescue of the crew and personally rescued three men, one of whom was seriously injured. During the following six days, he succeeded in getting his crew ashore, and after swimming many hours attempting to secure aid and food, finally effected the rescue of the men. His courage, endurance and excellent leadership contributed to the saving of several lives and was in keeping with the highest traditions of the United States Naval Service. "

CITATION FOR THE NAVY AND MARINE CORPS MEDAL
AWARDED TO JOHN F. KENNEDY

Captain Frederick Conklin congratulates
Lieutenant John F. Kennedy on the
awarding of the Navy and Marine Corps
Medal for his heroism during the PT
109 incident in August 1943, Chelsea
Hospital, Chelsea, Massachusetts,
June 11, 1944.

(ABOVE) Kathleen and her future husband, William (Billy) John Robert Cavendish, the Marquess of Hartington, heir to the Duke of Devonshire, circa 1943–1944.

(OPPOSITE) Jack and Kathleen in England, circa 1945.

(LEFT) Bobby, circa 1943–1944.

(BELOW) Bobby (center) with his classmates from the Navy V-12 program, circa 1944–1945.

(OPPOSITE) Bobby and a classmate from the Navy V-12 Program, circa 1944–1945.

The original photograph was inscribed: "Joe, as I knew him, in England, Aug 1944. Jim Simpson." This photograph was sent to the Kennedy family by Mr. Simpson [who served with Joe Jr. in England] after Joe's death.

❝ Joe did many things well, as his record illustrates, but I have always felt that Joe achieved his greatest success as the oldest brother. Very early in life he acquired a sense of responsibility towards his brothers and sisters, and I do not think that he ever forgot it. Towards me who was nearly his own age, this responsibility consisted in setting a standard that was uniformly high. For example, I never heard him utter a foul word or, until the last two or three years, ever swear. I suppose I knew Joe as well as anyone and yet, I sometimes wonder whether I ever really knew him. He had always a slight detachment from things around him—a wall of reserve which few people ever succeeded in penetrating. I do not mean by this that Joe was ponderous and heavy in his attitude. Far from it—I do not know anyone with whom I would rather have spent an evening or played golf or, in fact, done anything. He had a keen wit and saw the humorous side of people and situations quicker than anyone I have ever known.

313

He would spend long hours throwing a football with Bobby, swimming with Teddy, and teaching the younger girls how to sail. He was always close to Kick and was particularly close to her during some difficult times. I think that if the Kennedy children amount to anything now or ever amount to anything, it will be due more to Joe's behavior and his constant example than to any other factor. He made the task of bringing up a large family immeasurably easier for my father and mother for what they taught him, he passed on to us, and their teachings were not diluted through him, but rather strengthened

In appearance he resembled most his mother and he inherited from her a singular consideration and love for younger people and the gift of winning their affections immediately. From his father, Joe inherited a tremendous drive and capacity for work and a flowing and infectious vitality…

It is the realization that the future held the promise of great accomplishments for Joe that has made his death so particularly hard for those who knew him. His worldly success was so assured and inevitable that his death seems to have cut into the natural order of things. But at the same time, there is a completeness to Joe's life, and that is the completeness of perfection. His life as he lived and finally, as he died, could hardly have been improved upon…

He had great physical courage and stamina, a complete confidence in himself which never faltered, and he did everything with a great verve and gusto, and though these very qualities were in the end his undoing, yet they made his life a wonderful one to live.

And through it all, he had a deep and abiding Faith—he was never far from God—and so, I cannot help but feel that on that August day, high in the summer skies, 'death to him was less a setting forth than a returning.' **❞**

EXCERPT FROM JOHN F. KENNEDY'S ESSAY
"MY BROTHER JOE," FROM *AS WE REMEMBER JOE*

Jack with his Navy buddies. Back row: Red Fay, Jack,
Lenny Thom, Jim Reed, Barney Ross, and Bernie Lyons.
Front row: Teddy and Joey Gargan. Hyannis Port, Labor
Day weekend, September 1944.

Nancy Tenney, Pat, Eunice, Kathleen, Jean, Julia Reed,
and Kate Thom in Hyannis Port, Labor Day weekend,
September 1944.

Jack, Pat, Joe, Bobby, and Jean pose behind Rose (in kiddie pool) and Eunice in Palm Beach, circa 1944–1945.

CONGRATULATIONS:
HERE'S TO ALL THOSE 30 YEARS!
YOU'VE WASHED OUR HAIR AND CLEANED OUR EARS!
FOR 30 MORE JUST HAVE NO FEAR!
FOR WE'RE BEHIND YOU ALL NINE CHEERS!

POEM WRITTEN BY THE KENNEDY CHILDREN FOR THEIR PARENTS
ON THE OCCASION OF THEIR THIRTIETH WEDDING ANNIVERSARY

"For extraordinary heroism and courage in aerial flight as Pilot of a United States Navy Liberator Bomber on August 12, 1944. Well knowing the extreme dangers involved and totally unconcerned for his own safety, Lieutenant Kennedy unhesitatingly volunteered to conduct an exceptionally hazardous and special operational mission. Intrepid and daring in his tactics and with unwavering confidence in the vital importance of his task, he willingly risked his life in the supreme measure of service and, by his great personal valor and fortitude in carrying out a perilous undertaking, sustained and enhanced the finest traditions of the United States Naval Service."

CITATION FOR THE NAVY CROSS POSTHUMOUSLY
AWARDED TO JOSEPH P. KENNEDY JR.

(ABOVE) Pat, Jean, Joe, Teddy, Rose, and Eunice attend
the launching ceremony of the USS *Lt. Joseph P. Kennedy,
Jr.*, in Quincy, Massachusetts, July 26, 1945. Jean, Joe Jr.'s
goddaughter, christened the ship.

(OPPOSITE) At an award ceremony held in Boston on
June 27, 1945. Joseph P. Kennedy Jr. is posthumously
awarded the Navy Cross. Joe and Rose accept the medal
from Rear Admiral Felix Gygax as Pat, Teddy, Bobby,
and Jean look on.

Congressional candidate John F. Kennedy at the Bellevue Hotel seated under a shelf that holds photos of his parents, Joe and Rose, Boston, Massachusetts, 1946.

POLITICAL
BEGINNINGS

Joe Kennedy finally met with President Roosevelt in October 1944, and was "shocked beyond words" when he saw the president's physical deterioration. When he was asked to make a speech endorsing the president in the upcoming election that November, Joe's response was uncharacteristically terse and laden with sorrow: "With one son in the hospital, one son dead, and my son-in-law killed...I don't think it would be very helpful."

The war ended on August 14, 1945, when President Harry Truman announced that Japan had surrendered. By then Joe Kennedy was in semi-retirement, occasionally returning to public service, such as in September 1945, when Governor Maurice Tobin of Massachusetts invited Joe to become the "chairman of a commission to study the establishment of a state department of commerce," to help rejuvenate the state's economy.

As a private citizen, Joe founded the Joseph P. Kennedy Jr. Foundation in 1946 in memory of his late son, which in the beginning was created for the purpose of providing "relief, shelter, support, education, protection and maintenance of the indigent, sick or infirm." Jack served as the first president of the foundation.

After Joe Jr.'s death, Jack channeled his grief for his brother by collecting and editing a series of essays written by individuals who had known Joe Jr. during his lifetime. Privately printed in the spring of 1945, *As We Remember Joe* was Jack's loving tribute to his older brother. In addition to editing the memorial book, Jack was a Hearst correspondent at the United Na-

tions conference in San Francisco during the spring of 1945 and then returned to Great Britain for the first time since 1939 to report on the British elections. He also traveled to France, Germany, and Ireland, where he met Irish Prime Minister Éamon de Valera, with whom he struck up a friendship that lasted the rest of Jack's life. Still later, in July 1945, James Forrestal, the secretary of the Navy, invited Jack to accompany him to the Potsdam Conference in Berlin, Germany. At the time, Forrestal was interested in recruiting Jack for a position with the Navy Department. However, Jack had other ideas in regards to his future.

On April 22, 1946, Jack declared his candidacy for the Massachusetts Eleventh Congressional District, a seat once held by his grandfather, John "Honey Fitz" Fitzgerald. The whole Kennedy family supported Jack in his endeavor. Rose made campaign speeches on Jack's behalf throughout the eleventh district, and as a lifelong campaigner and a Gold Star Mother, she was instrumental in his success. Kennedy strategist Dave Powers wrote that "with the double-barreled name Fitzgerald and Kennedy she was better known than any in that 11th Congressional District...In

Bobby greets his father aboard the USS
Lt. Joseph P. Kennedy, Jr., April 12, 1946.

1946, she had a greater understanding of precinct politics than anyone in our organization." When Rose would finish speaking on the campaign trail, Powers noted, "she got a standing ovation."

Eunice, Pat, Bobby, and Jean worked in the campaign office and helped organize house parties where the constituents of the eleventh district could have an opportunity to meet and speak with Jack. Kick, who had remained in England after her husband's death, provided moral support from afar as did Teddy, who was then enrolled at Milton Academy in Massachusetts.

On June 19, 1946, the front page of the *Boston Daily Globe* declared, KENNEDY TOPS PRIMARY FIELD FOR CONGRESS. Jack won the Democratic nomination and then went on to defeat his Republican rival by a three-to-one margin. At age twenty-nine, Jack had reclaimed the Eleventh Congressional District seat that his grandfather, Honey Fitz, had held from 1895 to 1901, fortifying the connection to Boston that the family had never left behind, despite its sojourns around the world. Jack's decisive win in the November 1946 election began the next chapter in the Kennedy family history.

February 27th, 1946

" Motored down from Palm Beach to Colonel Clarke's house in Miami Beach to meet Mr. and Mrs. Winston Churchill and to watch the latter receive his degree from the University of Miami. Seymour Berry and I arrived about 9:15. Leslie Hore-Belisha and his wife, Cynthia were already there in the small living room of the house where the former Prime Minister was spending his vacation.

We hadn't been in the house long before Winston appeared downstairs with an enormous cigar, bare-footed in his dressing gown complaining as to whether quarter of ten meant quarter to or past. Mrs C. calmed him, he went upstairs and we (the party included General and Mrs. Anderson, Col. Clarke and Sarah Oliver) talked for about half an hour. Then escorted by 20 motor-cycle policemen we drove to the Orange Bowl Stadium.

We marched in the official entourage followed by members of different Florida universities. I sat on the platform in between Seymour and L. Hore-Belisha. Afterwards we drove back to the Clarkes, picked up our suits and bathed at the Surf Club.

Winston presented a very comical sight bobbing around in the surf. He adores the water although I must say I wouldn't enjoy swimming in quite such a public spot every day. He asked about Daddy and when I said he sends you best regards W.C. replied 'he makes an exception in my case.' Daddy took umbrage at this remark. We then all went upstairs for the big official luncheon. I sat at the main table next to John Erskine who wrote 'Private Life of Helen of Troy' which supposedly made him an expert on the subject of women. There were about 20 short speeches and we arose from lunch about 4:00 P.M.

Mrs. Churchill is so gracious and with overwhelming charm. "

EXCERPT FROM KATHLEEN KENNEDY HARTINGTON'S DIARY, FEBRUARY 27, 1946

Kathleen with Sir Winston Churchill, in Miami, Florida, February 27, 1946.

The Kennedy family in Hyannis Port, circa 1946. Back
row: Joe, Teddy, Pat, and Bobby. Front row: Rose, Jean,
Eunice, Kathleen, and Jack.

Kathleen and Eunice, circa 1946.

Bobby, Jean, and Teddy in Hyannis Port, circa 1945–1946.

Eunice, Jack, Moe, and Teddy, circa 1946.

"One of Jack's dogs was a Doberman Pinscher called Moe. Jack was in Arizona for his health and living in a rather remote place and bought the dog both for company and as a watchdog. Then he moved on someplace where he couldn't take the dog, so he shipped him home. It was supposed to be for Mother's birthday, or something like that. The dog arrived one day on the front porch in a big slatted, open crate with a big sign on it: MY NAME IS MOE AND I DON'T BITE. Everybody gathered around, and Teddy opened the door of the crate and the dog jumped out and bit him. He immediately sent a telegram to Jack: 'THIS DOG THAT DOESN'T BITE JUST JUMPED OUT OF HIS CAGE AND BIT ME. TEDDY' "

PAT REMEMBERS MOE, HER BROTHER JACK'S DOBERMAN PINSCHER

Teddy and Jack prepare to go sailing in Hyannis Port, circa 1946.

Ted Williams, Eddie Pellagrini, Jack, and Hank Green-
berg at Fenway Park, Boston, Massachusetts, April 1946.

Jack has dinner with his family, friends, and campaign workers, 1946. Seated left to right: Francis X. Morrissey, Mary Josephine Fitzgerald, Eunice (center), Jack, Honey Fitz, and Joseph F. Timilty. Lem Billings is standing behind Mary Josephine. Kenny O'Donnell and Helen Sullivan (the future Mrs. O'Donnell) are standing behind Jack and Honey Fitz.

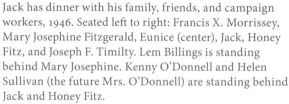

" Dearest Jack,

This letter has been coming for ages. It's just to tell you how terrifically pleased I am for you. Everyone says you were so good in the Election and the outcome must have been a great source of satisfaction. It's nice to know you are as appreciated in the 11th Congressional District as you are among your brothers & sisters. Gee, aren't you lucky?

…Write soon 4 Smith Square S.W.1. and my best love to you from

Kick **"**

**EXCERPT FROM KATHLEEN KENNEDY HARTINGTON'S LETTER
TO HER BROTHER JACK, JULY 13, 1946**

Jack marches in a 1946 parade during his first campaign
for the Massachusetts Eleventh Congressional District.

Jack makes a speech before a women's group during
the 1946 primary election. Rose is seated on the platform
to the left.

Jack, accompanied by his grandparents Mary Josephine
(center) and Honey Fitz, votes in the 1946 primary
election, June 18, 1946.

"The star of Jack's first campaign for Congress in 1946 was Rose Kennedy. She had a great understanding of Ward and Precinct politics, having accompanied her father John F. 'Honey Fitz' Fitzgerald through the 22 Wards of Boston in his bid for re-election as Mayor of Boston in 1910…

She warmed up the crowd until it was Jack's turn to speak. She charmed them with stories about bringing up nine children. She carried 3×5 cards with records of visits to the doctor or dentist.

One evening at a rally at the Veterans of Foreign Wars Hall in Brighton, the crowd packed the hall and loud speakers were set up outside to handle the hundreds who wanted to listen. Jack was running late and Rose was shuffling the cards a second time. A member of Jack's campaign committee had advised Jack to wear a soft hat as he campaigned so he would look a little older. When Jack finally arrived, he approached his mother and said, 'Mother, how do I look in a hat?' She said, 'You would have looked much better to me an hour ago.'"

DAVE POWERS'S RECOLLECTIONS
OF ROSE KENNEDY'S CAMPAIGN SKILLS

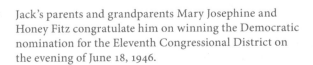

Jack's parents and grandparents Mary Josephine and Honey Fitz congratulate him on winning the Democratic nomination for the Eleventh Congressional District on the evening of June 18, 1946.

(ABOVE) Jack, flanked by Rose and Joe, on the night
he won the Democratic nomination for the Eleventh
Congressional District.

(OPPOSITE) A congratulatory telegram from Honey
Fitz to Jack on the day Jack is to be sworn in as the
U.S. Representative from Massachusetts, Eleventh
Congressional District.

CLASS OF SERVICE
This is a full-rate Telegram or Cablegram unless its deferred character is indicated by a suitable symbol above or preceding the address.

WESTERN UNION

JOSEPH L. EGAN
PRESIDENT

1201

(08)
1-2

SYMBOLS
DL=Day Letter
NL=Night Letter
LC=Deferred Cable
NLT=Cable Night Letter
Ship Radiogram

The filing time shown in the date line on telegrams and day letters is STANDARD TIME at point of origin. Time of receipt is STANDARD TIME at point of destination

WA130 39=BOSTON MASS 3 1057A

1947 JAN 3 PM 12 10

JOHN F KENNEDY=

HOUSE OF REPRESENTATIVES=

=INCREDIBLY BAD WEATHER CONDITIONS HAVE MADE IT INADVISABLE FOR ME TO ATTEMPT TRIP TO WASHINGTON MAY TODAY MARK THE BEGINNING OF SERVICE THAT WILL MAKE YOUR NAME SOME DAY A HOUSEHOLD WORD THROUGHOUT THE COUNTRY FEELING PRETTY GOOD.

GRANDPA=

JOHN F FITZGERALD.

THE COMPANY WILL APPRECIATE SUGGESTIONS FROM ITS PATRONS CONCERNING ITS SERVICE

ACKNOWLEDGMENTS

This book is a labor of love by many people. First, by my grandparents, who took, organized, and collected countless photographs of their large family. The staff of the Kennedy Library has worked incredibly hard over the years to preserve and catalogue this collection and make it available in this beautiful book. And the people at Hachette Book Group's Grand Central Publishing who have been involved in this publication took on an immense task and have executed it brilliantly. So many individuals made a special effort, and some of them deserve special thanks here.

First, I would like to thank my aunt, Ambassador Jean Kennedy Smith, without whose support this book would not have been published. I would also like to thank my cousin Tom Fitzgerald for letting us excerpt from his collection of family reminiscences. And a special nod to my cousins, who have shared their parents' notes, photos, and memories in this book.

At the John F. Kennedy Library Foundation, which shares all proceeds from the publication of these photographs with the Joseph P. Kennedy Jr. Foundation, Jennifer Quan has been the indispensable woman. She has spent the past several years researching and selecting the photos and compiling their descriptions. She has been championed by Tom McNaught, the Foundation's wonderful executive director, and supported by Doris Drummond, Karen Mullen, and Rachel Flor—the Dream Team among presidential library foundations.

The JFK Presidential Library and Museum is part of the National Archives and Records Administration, whose staff works tirelessly to preserve history and make my father's legacy available to new generations. We are fortunate to have the support of David Ferriero, Archivist of the United States, and to be led by Director Tom Putnam and Chief Archivist Karen Adler-Abramson, whose staff provided invaluable assistance on this project. In particular, the staff of the Audiovisual Archives—Laurie Austin, James Hill, and Maryrose Grossman and former interns Sara Ludovissy and Catherine Robertson—helped with scanning and identifying images. This book benefitted greatly from the knowledge and experience of Allan Goodrich, the Library's former chief archivist, who shepherded this collection from my grandmother's house to the Library and oversaw it for many years.

Other departments of the Library also assisted with this project—namely Stephen Plotkin, Sharon Kelly, Michael Desmond, and Stacey Chandler of the Research Room, who helped place the images in their historical context, and Sam Rubin in the Education Department, who made sure every detail was accurate.

The book is greatly enriched by the introductory essays by Michael Quinlin, whose knowledge of the Boston Irish experience is unparalleled, and by the advice and direction of historian Ellen Fitzpatrick.

We are especially grateful to Robert Bachrach of Bachrach Photographers, who generously allowed us to use his studio's iconic images of my family over the years.

And a shout-out to Steve Eidelman, the executive director of the Joseph P. Kennedy Jr. Foundation, whose commitment to the intellectually disabled and service to the Foundation is truly a blessing.

At Grand Central Publishing, I would like to thank Jamie Raab and Deb Futter for believing wholeheartedly in this project. Thanks to Allyson Rudolph; Thomas Whatley in production; Carolyn Kurek and Bob Castillo in managing editorial; and Anne Twomey and Claire Brown in art. Also thanks to Emi Battaglia, Matthew Ballast, and Jimmy Franco in marketing and publicity for spreading the word.

This book would not have happened without the vision, commitment, and perseverance of Gretchen Young, who has worked with the Library on four books. Gretchen's commitment to excellence and her refusal to settle for anything less has inspired me throughout the ten books we have done together. She shares that passion with Shubhani Sarkar, whose truly beautiful design helps bring these photos to life.

As always, I am grateful to Esther Newberg and John Delaney for helping the Library find wonderful partners in publishing, and seeing us through all the twists and turns that have come our way.

—CAROLINE KENNEDY

CREDITS

PHOTOS

Lem Billings. Lem Billings Trip Book, John F. Kennedy Presidential Library. Page 192.

Boston Globe. Original 1979 JFKL Museum Exhibit, JFKL. Page 33.

Boston Herald. Boston Herald Collection, JFKL. Pages 20, 38.

Corbis. Pages 201, 212, 214–215, 259.

Copyright Caroline Kennedy. Jacqueline Kennedy Onassis Collection, JFKL. Pages 136 (top), 205, 234, 236–237, 248, 290, 316–317.

Kennedy Family Collection, JFKL. Pages 1–2, 6, 8, 10–12, 15–16, 17 (top), 19, 21–25, 27, 39–42, 44–51, 55–58, 60–67, 69–80, 82, 86, 89–92, 95–114, 124–125, 135, 136 (bottom), 137–140, 142–145, 147–148, 150–157, 163–172, 175–179, 182–183, 185–188, 190–191, 197, 202, 208, 213, 216–221, 223, 227, 229, 244, 246–247, 251, 253–254, 260, 265, 269–274, 276, 283–287, 289, 295–298, 299 (left), 300, 304, 308–310, 312, 324, 326–327, 329–331, 337, 340.

Courtesy of Bachrach. Kennedy Family Collection, JFKL. Pages 30, 37, 43, 52.

Bethlehem Steel Company. Kennedy Family Collection, JFKL. Page 311.

Conlin. Kennedy Family Collection, JFKL. Title page, pages 9, 17 (bottom), 28.

E. F. Foley. Kennedy Family Collection, JFKL. Page 123.

McClellan Studios. Kennedy Family Collection, JFKL. Page 134.

Richard Sears. Kennedy Family Collection, JFKL. Pages 126–133.

United States Navy. Kennedy Family Collection, JFKL. Pages 292–294, 318–319.

President's Collection, JFKL. Pages 68, 180–181, 193–194, 198, 207, 226, 238–239, 243, 252, 256–257, 291, 299 (right), 301, 303, 307, 314–315, 328, 332–336, 338–339, 342.

Felici. President's Collection, JFKL. Pages 230–231.

Frank Turgeon. President's Collection, JFKL. Page 262.

United States Navy. President's Collection, JFKL. Page 323.

PX65-25, JFKL. Page 240–241.

Courtesy of Bachrach. Bachrach Collection, JFKL. Pages iv–v, 158–160.

Original 1979 JFKL Museum Exhibit, JFKL. Page 5.

Time–Life/Getty. Page 320.

DOCUMENTS

Page 34 Wedding Announcement of Rose Fitzgerald and Joseph P. Kennedy, Rose Fitzgerald Kennedy Papers, John F. Kennedy Presidential Library.

Page 36 "The Wedding Log," 1914: October 7–28, "The Wedding Log," Series 1: Diaries, 1908–1975, ROFKPP, Box 1, John F. Kennedy Presidential Library.

Page 67 Letter, John F. Kennedy to Rose Kennedy, December 29, 1924, 1923–1927, Series 1.1 Family Correspondence, 1923–1968, Joseph P. Kennedy Personal Papers, Box 1, JFKL.

Page 73 Telegram, Joseph P. Kennedy Sr. to Edward Moore, August 28, 1926, ROFKPP, JFKL.

Page 83 Telegram, Joseph P. Kennedy Sr. to John F. Kennedy, May 19, 1926, Letters, cards, report card & drawings, 1918–1928, Series 7.7 John F. Kennedy, 1917–1980, ROFKPP, Box 127, JFKL.

Page 84–85 Letter, Joseph P. Kennedy Sr. to Rose Kennedy, circa 1925, Joseph P. Kennedy letters to family members, 1925–1940, undated, Series 3.5 Family Correspondence File, 1910–1994, ROFKPP, Box 55, JFKL.

Page 94 Rose Fitzgerald Kennedy Papers, John F. Kennedy Presidential Library.

Page 115–117 Letter, John F. Kennedy to Joseph P. Kennedy Sr., February 25, 1929, reprinted with permission.

Page 118–119 Letter, John F. Kennedy to Rose Kennedy, circa 1930–1931, Correspondence, 1929–1935, Series 2 Early Years, 1928–1940, John F. Kennedy Personal Papers, Box 1, JFKL.

Page 120–121 Letter, John F. Kennedy to Rose Kennedy, circa November 1930, reprinted with permission.

Page 126 "A Plea for a Raise," Correspondence, 1929–1935, Series 2 Early Years, 1928–1940, JFKPP, Box 1, JFKL.

Page 135 Letter, John F. Kennedy to Rose Kennedy, undated, Correspondence, 1929–1935, Series 2 Early Years, 1928–1940, JFKPP, Box 1, JFKL.

Page 137 Letter, Joseph P. Kennedy Jr. to Joseph P. Kennedy Sr. and Rose Kennedy, February 5, 1933, Joseph P. Kennedy Jr., Family Correspondence, 1926–1940, undated, Series 2.3 Background Materials, 1908–1982, ROFKPP, Box 12, JFKL.

Page 141 (top) Choate School Report of John F. Kennedy in History, Fourth Quarter, reprinted with permission.

Page 141 (bottom) Choate School Report of John F. Kennedy in his House, Fourth Quarter, Correspondence, 1929–1935, Series 2 Early Years, 1928–1940, JFKPP, Box 1, JFKL.

Page 149 "A Fish Story," Robert F. Kennedy, April 1934, "School Life," 1934, Series 7.12 Robert F. Kennedy, 1935–1950, 1961–1972, ROFKPP, Box 129, JFKL.

Page 186 Letter, Eunice Kennedy to Joseph P. Kennedy Sr. and Rose Kennedy, July 13, Eunice Kennedy: Family Correspondence, 1928–1958, Series 2.3 Background Materials, 1908–1982, ROFKPP, Box 13, JFKL.

Page 192 Excerpts from Lem Billings Trip Book dated July 31, 1937, August 4, 1937, and August 15, 1937, Billings Trip Book, PX93-34, JFKL.

Page 196 Letter, Edward M. Kennedy to Santa Claus, undated, Letters for Chapter 14,

1939–1940, Series 2.3 Background Materials, 1908–1982, ROFKPP, Box 15, JFKL.

Page 206 Diary entries dated February 18, 1938, February 23, 1938, and March 8, 1938, Diary, February–December 1938, Folder 1 of 4, Series 8.1 Appointments & Diary, 1938–1951, JPKPP, Box 100, JFKL.

Page 209–211 Letter, Patricia Kennedy to Joseph P. Kennedy Sr., January 19, 1938, Children: Daughters, 1938–1958, Series 3.5 Family Correspondence File, 1910–1994, ROFKPP, Box 55, JFKL.

Page 222 Letter, Robert F. Kennedy to Joseph P. Kennedy Sr., December 11, 1938, 1938–1942, Series 1.1 Family Correspondence, 1923–1968, JPKPP, Box 2, JFKL.

Page 224–225 Letter, Eunice Kennedy to Joseph P. Kennedy Sr., December 26, 1938, 1938–1942, Series 1.1 Family Correspondence, 1923–1968, JPKPP, Box 2, JFKL.

Page 227 Letter, Rose Kennedy to Mary Josephine Fitzgerald, undated, Rose Kennedy's letters to her mother, [father and brothers]: From the American Embassy [London], 1938, Series 2.3 Background Materials, 1908–1982, ROFKPP, Box 12, JFKL.

Page 228 Diary entries dated January 7, 1939 and January 10, 1939, Edward M. Kennedy Diary, Kennedy Family Collection, JFKL.

Page 232 Diary entry dated March 13, 1939, Edward M. Kennedy Diary, KFC, JFKL.

Page 233 Diary entry dated March 13, 1939, Diary, February–December 1939, Folder 1 of 4, Series 8.1 Appointments & Diary, 1938–1951, JPKPP, Box 100, JFKL.

Page 235 Diary entry dated March 16, 1939, Edward M. Kennedy Diary, KFC, JFKL.

Page 236 Diary entry dated March 15, 1939, February–December 1939, Folder 1 of 4, Series 8.1 Appointments & Diary, 1938–1951, JPKPP, Box 100, JFKL.

Page 237 Diary entry dated March 14, 1939, Edward M. Kennedy Diary, KFC, JFKL.

Page 245 Letter, Joseph P. Kennedy Sr. to Edward M. Kennedy, September 11, 1940, Edward M. Kennedy: Family Correspondence, 1935–1962, undated, Series 2.3 Background Materials, 1908–1982, ROFKPP, Box 14, JFKL.

Page 261 Letter, Joseph P. Kennedy Sr. to Rose Kennedy, September 30, 1940, Rose Kennedy, Personal, 1910–1959, undated, Series 3.5 Family Correspondence File, 1910–1994, ROFKPP, Box 55, JFKL.

Page 271 (bottom) Diary entry dated May 22, 1941, Diary, "Married Life," 1914–1944, Series 2.3 Background Materials, 1908–1982, ROFKPP, Box 12, JFKL.

Page 277–281 Letter, Patricia Kennedy to John F. Kennedy, July 10, 1942, Children, 1926–1944, Series 3.5 Family Correspondence File, 1910–1994, ROFKPP, Box 55, JFKL.

Page 282 (top) Letter, Rose Kennedy to Kennedy Children, January 5, 1941, Children 1926–1944, Series 3.5 Family Correspondence File, 1910–1994, ROFKPP, Box 55, JFKL.

Page 282 (bottom) Letter, Rose Kennedy to Kennedy Children, January 12, 1942, Children 1926–1944, Series 3.5 Family Correspondence File, 1910–1994, ROFKPP, Box 55, JFKL.

Page 287 Letter, Rose Kennedy to Kennedy Children, March 27, 1942, Children 1926–1944, Series 3.5 Family Correspondence File, 1910–1994, ROFKPP, Box 55, JFKL.

Page 288 Rose Fitzgerald Kennedy Papers, John F. Kennedy Presidential Library.

Page 296 Letter, Kathleen Kennedy to John F. Kennedy, undated, Correspondence with friends and family, 1941–1946, Series 7.9 Kathleen Kennedy Hartington, 1928–1946, 1969–1976, ROFKPP, Box 128, JFKL.

Page 297 Letter, Rose Kennedy to Kennedy Children, May 13, 1943, 1943: January–October, Series 1.1 Family Correspondence, 1923–1968, JPKPP, Box 2, JFKL.

Page 300 Letter, John F. Kennedy to Joseph P. Kennedy Sr. and Rose Kennedy, August 12, 1943, John F. Kennedy, August–September 1943, Series 3.5 Family Correspondence File, 1910–1994, ROFKPP, Box 56, JFKL.

Page 302 Letter, Rose Kennedy to Kennedy Children, January 31, 1944, Children, 1926–1944,

Series 3.5 Family Correspondence File, 1910–1994, ROFKPP, Box 55, JFKL.

Page 305 Letter, Joseph P. Kennedy Jr. to Patricia Kennedy, December 11, 1943, Children: Daughters, 1938–1958, Series 3.5 Family Correspondence File, 1910–1994, ROFKPP, Box 55, JFKL.

Page 306 (top) Letter, Lt. A. P. Cluster to Joseph P. Kennedy Sr., January 9, 1944, Kennedy, Joseph P. Sr.: General Correspondence, 1940–1946, Series 5.1 Correspondence, 1933–1950: Family, JFKPP, Box 4, JFKL.

Page 306 (bottom) Citation, Officer Selection Board Jacket, Series 8 Naval Records, JFKPP, Box 11B, JFKL.

Page 317 Telegrams to Mrs. Kennedy, Rose Kennedy, Personal, undated, Series 3.5 Family Correspondence File, 1910–1994, ROFKPP, Box 55, JFKL.

Page 325 Diary entry dated February 27, 1946, Kathleen Kennedy Hartington Diary, KFC, JFKL.

Page 331 Rose Fitzgerald Kennedy Papers, John F. Kennedy Presidential Library.

Page 336 Letter, Kathleen Kennedy Hartington to John F. Kennedy, July 13, 1946, Kennedy, Kathleen: Correspondence, 1942–1947 and undated, Series 5.1 Correspondence: 1933–1950: Family, JFKPP, Box 4, JFKL.

Page 343 Telegram, John F. Fitzgerald to John F. Kennedy, January 3, 1947, Family, 1947, Series 6 Correspondence, 1943–1952, JFKPP, Box 5, JFKL.

BOOKS

Items appearing on pages 81 and 268
Fitzgerald, Jr., Thomas A. *Grandpa Stories.*
Rundel Park Press, 2006.

Items appearing on pages 22, 42, 136, 195, 258, 271 (top) and 341
Kennedy, Edward M. *Her Grace Above Gold.*
Salem, Massachusetts: Deschamps Printing Company, Inc., 1997.

Items appearing on pages 313 and 318
Kennedy, John F. *As We Remember Joe.* Cambridge, Massachusetts: University Press, 1945.

Items appearing on pages xiii, 8, 10, 13, 18, 23, 25, 38, 39, 68, 71, 138, 249 (top), and 273
Kennedy, Rose Fitzgerald. *Times to Remember.* Garden City, New York: Doubleday & Company, Inc., 1974.

Items appearing on pages 93, 220, 249 (bottom), and 275
Smith, Amanda. *Hostage to Fortune: The Letters of Joseph P. Kennedy.* New York, New York: Viking, 2001.

I SHALL PASS THROUGH THIS WORLD BUT ONCE.
ANY KINDNESS I CAN DO,
OR GOODNESS SHOW, LET ME DO IT NOW—
FOR I SHALL NOT PASS THIS WAY AGAIN.

This Quaker maxim hung on a plaque over
Patrick Joeseph Kennedy's desk.